BIM
FOR DESIGN FIRMS

BIM

FOR DESIGN FIRMS
*data rich architecture at
small and medium scales*

FRANÇOIS LÉVY AND JEFFREY W. OUELLETTE

WILEY

Registered Office
John Wiley & Sons, Inc., 111 River Street, Hoboken, NJ 07030, USA

Editorial Office
111 River Street, Hoboken, NJ 07030, USA

For details of our global editorial offices, customer services, and more information about Wiley products visit us at www.wiley.com.

Wiley also publishes its books in a variety of electronic formats and by print-on-demand. Some content that appears in standard print versions of this book may not be available in other formats.

Library of Congress Cataloging-in-Publication Data is Available:

ISBN 9781119252801 (Hardback)
ISBN 9781119252818 (ePDF)
ISBN 9781119252832 (ePub)

Cover Design: Wiley
Cover Image: © SPLANN, lead architect Hamonic+Masson & Associes with A/LTA, associate architect

Set in 11/13pt and AntiqueOliveStd by SPi-Global, Chennai, India

V10011789_070219

For Julie

In the 1995 movie *Get Shorty*, Delroy Lindo, in the role of Bo Catlett, says, "You have an idea, you write down what you wanna say. Then you get somebody to add in the commas . . . if you aren't positive yourself . . . you come to the last page you write . . . The End." Would that writing were so simple or straightforward! This book has taken far longer than I had initially anticipated or hoped, in spite of it's not being my first rodeo. Any project of such a span has countless benefactors and supporters, some whose names appear in these pages, and many who have contributed less apparently. A heartfelt thanks and appreciation to the many architects, designers, educators, and photographers who contributed case studies, images, and ideas to this book, in particular Justin Dowhower and my co-author Jeffrey Ouellette, who made substantial contributions to the manuscript. To Mark Winford, thank you for your early partnership, for Mosaic, and our projects together. I'd also like to extend thanks to all my friends and colleagues at Vectorworks, and especially Robert Anderson, Sarah Barrett, and Rubina Siddiqui who contributed images or helped me think through certain ideas.

I owe a deep debt of thanks to Kimberly Kohlhaas, my design and business partner of several years, many of whose own contributions have influenced my design thinking and our firm's projects that appear here. To our staff, current and past, I am grateful for your hard work, intelligence, and heart: Sherri Woolley Ancipink, Christopher Balli, Charlton Lewis, and Barrett Webb. And while many project renderings are shown in the following pages, these are real projects for real clients, most of whom I have the privilege to call friends. Their genuine trust in our firm has been a source of professional satisfaction and personal joy. Thank you Adam, Megan, Marlon, Jennifer, Dan, Laura, Jörg, Nancy, Jana, Lex, Jake, Joy, Steve, Dave, Tim, Katie, Alice, Diane, Mike, Sanjay, Mandy, Jan, Stanley, Catherine, and Larry. I'd like to thank the dedicated, hardworking, and patient people at Wiley, particularly Helen Castle, Margaret Cummins, Vishnu Narayanan, Kalli Schultea, and Jayalakshmi Erkathil Thevarkandi.

Finally, this is a bittersweet opportunity to express my profound gratitude and appreciation for the late Constance Adams. While not a "BIM" architect, she was a brilliant visionary whose trust and confidence in me never flagged.

François Lévy

My contribution is only possible because of the collective kindness and knowledge of a great number of people—teachers, mentors, family, friends (and competitors!), employers, customers, and collaborators—inspiring me to be a conduit, an advocate, a champion, for their best ideas. I'd especially like to thank François for asking me to be a part of this endeavor. Over the years, he's been a peer, colleague, boss, customer, and most importantly, a friend. I really appreciate his confidence in me to be a part of another one of his illuminative projects.

Jeffrey Ouellette

This is a personal book. It is largely informed by my career in architecture to date, the lessons I have discovered about the process of design, the mistakes I have made, and the colleagues, clients, and students from whom I have learned. It is anecdotal, which is not to say that it is not factual nor accurate. It hopes to be conversational in tone, and perhaps entertaining. Certainly I have enjoyed sharing what I have come to know and believe about BIM (building information modeling). Before the term had been coined, I had begun to use a BIM process— albeit one higher on building modeling and lighter on information. In part this was motivated out of a sense of adventurousness, but primarily it seemed to be a promising methodology to explore design opportunities, from novel geometry to the quantitative analysis of thermal chimneys and rainwater harvesting. At the time much of the parametrization of BIM tools was yet to come, so many model elements had to be assembled from scratch from 3D primitives (extrusions, sweeps, Boolean additives, and so forth). Even then, it was clear that there were new designs possible that would not have been previously feasible to explore.

Through no virtue of mine, I have been fortunate in my timing. I happened to enter the profession of architecture at a time when computational power began to become ubiquitously available. In college I had written my senior thesis on a friend's TRS-80, and its great graphical upgrade consisted of an amber screen (easier on the eyes than white letters on a black background) and letter descenders (like the tail in the letter g) that could be displayed below the line, instead of g's, j's, and q's being vertically compressed and moved up, like this: mʏ ϙuixotic ϱuest is a ɟudɠe. By the time I was a graduate student in architecture school, CAD was available on desktop computers, rather than dedicated draft- ing stations that combined hardware and software in one inseparable package. By the time I was working in a firm, the earliest versions of what was to come to be called BIM were available. I've been very lucky to have seen the profession span from hand drafting to CAD to BIM, and having the first-hand experience of working across those technologies has been highly instructional.

Richard Dodge and the Virtual Making of Things

In 1992 I was a graduate student in the first design studio that was CADD-based (computer-aided design and drafting) at the University of Texas at Austin School of Architecture, taught by the late Richard Dodge. The story I heard was that Richard's father had been a builder in California, and the younger Dodge had been drafting (on a table of course, with a parallel bar and triangles) since his teens. By the time Richard was an architect he could draft like an angel with the speed of a bullet. So it may have seemed odd that he embraced CADD as he did, but he was like that: a frank and engaging professor, an accomplished and intellectually curious designer, a technically proficient architect who was no less talented for being so professionally grounded.

I remember one day in studio a conversation about the connection between drawing and making. Richard suggested that the day was already here when our architectural drawings could directly drive machines to manufacture custom building components that would otherwise be cost-prohibitive to fabricate by hand. Numerically controlled (NC) milling machines had been around in the manufacturing world since the 1950s, computer numerically controlled (CNC) routers were already in use. But it hadn't occurred to us that the technology of mass manufacturing could literally be at our fingertips. The limitation wasn't the milling machines, of course. The bottleneck was the architect not having a ready medium to communicate with the CNC router—until ubiquitous CADD (Figure I.1). Even then, my imagination was limited to structurally expressive wood truss gusset plates, or heroic steel clevises that one might find on Lloyd's of London or the Centre Pompidou (what my grandfather like many Parisians called *Notre-Dame-des-Tuyaux*—Our Lady of the Tubes). Additive manufacturing machines (3D printers) were obscure enough to still be science fiction to most of us.

Yet in that far-ranging conversation, sprawling from the charcoal pencil drawing technology of the Baroque to the precision mechanical drafting of the modernists, we could see the outlines of virtual buildings through the fog of the future. We imagined what it might mean once we were given license to draw not just a select few plans, sections, and elevations, but model an entire building virtually. We could not predict what was to come, but we did see that the nature of the tools that we used to design and document our buildings would change the very expression of those buildings. Just as the Baroque could not be Baroque without charcoal, nor modernism without technical drafting pens, so too our coming architecture would be an expression of our digital tools. We knew that the tools we would come to use would shape that which they wrought, and all we had was a choice: be open-eyed about that relationship, or stick our heads in the sand.

FIGURE I.1 An early CADD drawing. The truss design is predicated on the assumption that that the plywood gusset plates would be fabricated with a CNC machine, laid out on a sheet to minimize material waste.

BIM for Studios

Most of my professional experience is in small firms, and as a consequence the BIM design praxis that I have learned and developed evolved around smaller projects with fewer designers. So there's a certain logic for the title of this book to reference that perspective. "Architecture" is of course my profession. Let's not forget that there are many other disciplines that employ BIM and that architects were hardly the first to embrace it, putting it mildly. "Data-rich" suggests that BIM is employed for analytical computational design and simulation. That is, there is a performative implication to the use of BIM for design.

Since its inception, BIM has been assumed to primarily be the sandbox of large firms and their large-scale projects. That's understandable. First, the extent and complexity of large projects has made them low-hanging fruit, ripe for a new way of drawing and collaborating to help manage the considerable human capital and information required to design and document them. Moreover, software, hardware, and training costs associated with the revolutionary new technology to support BIM can arguably be more easily absorbed by large firms than small ones. One of BIM's important features is its ability to foster interoperability between various design and building professions; large projects tend to have more players at the design table, so to speak, than smaller ones.

BIM has long been touted for benefits to documentation and coordination. As a digital artifact, the building information model is developed by one or more design disciplines—architectural, structural, mechanical, and so forth—each contributing assemblies or components to (a) federated model(s). As a process, building information model*ing* assumes an exchange of information in order to establish the geometry and characteristics of a proposed project based on each design stakeholder's respective contribution. The process requires defined and delineated roles, interoperable data exchange formats, coordination, and communication. The model may evolve through late-stage design processes through these exchange procedures, but it is presupposed that there is already a design to begin with. That is, the BIM process is the social and technological protocol by which the BIM artifact progresses as a concerted digital response to an established architectural design.

As a practitioner, while some of my experiences are congruent with the above, on the whole my BIM life has been swimming against the general current. With some exceptions, most of my design collaborators do not use BIM, so projects tend to involve a single model rather than a federated one from multiple professional stakeholders. Even then, there are opportunities for BIM coordination with collaborators (see case studies from Chapters 5 and 6). Over the past two decades, my professional experience has been in firms of one to five, well within the bounds of the definition of "small firms" (years ago, the Boston Society of Architects reported perhaps anecdotally that 80% of architects worked in firms of six or fewer; see Figure I.2). And while I enjoy BIM's significant productivity gains in all phases of design including construction documents, BIM has not been relegated to merely documentation and coordination. Indeed, it is in large part this inversion of the typical BIM use case that has led to this book. BIM for design and BIM for a small firm is almost the antithesis of BIM as it is frequently deployed for documentation and coordination of large projects.

And in spite of that, I would contend that BIM for design and in small teams is not antithetical to large firms. True, interoperability is especially critical on large projects to automate the coordination of architecture with site, civil, structural, mechanical, electrical, and plumbing engineering disciplines. Yet the design benefits of a broader, data-rich 3D design process—as distinct from that subset of design comprised of coordination and construction documentation—can be reaped by studios within larger firms. Even large architecture firms create manageable team sizes to design and develop architectural projects. Fueled in part

FIGURE I.2 As of 2010, there were just under 104,000 registered architects in the continental United States, according to NCARB. Each blue dot represents about 100 US architects; each red dot roughly represents 100 architects in firms of more than 6. Dot distribution is entirely random within each state, and red dot distribution is approximate.

by technological advances and increased personal productivity, the trend for creating formal or informal small design studios within larger firms is palpable. This book is for them, too.

A Horse of a Different Color

Here's a common story about design; tell me if it sounds familiar. After a flurry of parti diagrams and inspired sketches, and on the heels of code research and programming, a project is conceptually developed using sketch modeling software. It gets refined, perhaps exported to rendering software for initial client meetings, postprocessed by a Photoshop wunderkind. Eventually the schematic design matures, and it's time to get serious about building systems and preliminary structural coordination. So the model is rebuilt using BIM authoring software, and rolls along in design development. Then the deadline looms, and half the project is hurriedly drafted in 2D CADD while some of the BIM model limps gamely across the finish line. At each step of the way, of course, data is lost as the project is exported from one software platform to another, with frequent redoing of completed work. And if there were significant design changes in design development or construction documents, backtracking created more inefficiencies.

So even in those firms that have arrogated BIM, that adoption may not be with as much depth as might be expected. Indeed, large firms that adopt BIM may be more prone to a cobbled approach to design and production software tools. Not that there's a moral virtue to a "full BIM" ethic, nor is there any particular value in being dogmatic for dogmatism's sake (indeed I tend to find the opposite). Rather, the pressure to get work produced and meet deadlines can place short-term expediency at odds with best practices, and as a result there are missed opportunities for exploring and resolving alternative design possibilities.

It is beyond question in my experience that BIM is a more efficient way to work. That is, less effort (as measured in time devoted to delivering architectural

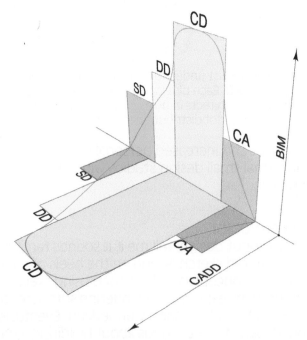

FIGURE I.3 The BIM gap: CADD versus BIM. In CADD (and manual drafting), less time can be devoted to earlier design phases since construction documentation (CD) comprises around 40% of architectural services (graphed on ground plane). In BIM (upright), not only are CDs a smaller portion of overall services, but throughout design and documentation architectural services are more efficient with BIM (blue curve) than CADD (red curve). One possible benefit of this *efficiency* windfall is to devote more design effort to architectural *effectiveness*.

services) is required with BIM to produce an equivalent instrument of service (i.e., set of architectural documents) as would be produced with CADD (see Figure I.3). But efficiency only expresses the ratio of effort to output. It says nothing about effectiveness—the degree to which the output produces desirable results. Effectiveness is a measure of success.

At its most orthodox, BIM is about efficiency. Perhaps a question worth asking is, "To what end?" I propose that we reinvest those efficiency gains in effective architecture. In other words, let's design more: design more deeply, design more thoughtfully, design more courageously. *BIM for Design Studios Firms* is intended to help unearth alternative design possibilities and point to new opportunities for architects and designers to exploit BIM for far more than executing designs whose conclusions are already baked in. This book is not about "faster, better CADD." It's not a software manual, nor a handbook of tips and tricks to improve efficiency, nor a primer for BIM managers. It is a guide to investigate something new about design, suggesting that technique and methodology are intimately bound to architecture.

François Lévy, AIA
Austin, Texas

BIM
FOR DESIGN FIRMS

What is design? Is there a particular quality to digital design processes?

A question asked with the objective of obtaining a definitive answer is not a very interesting question. A question asked in an open-ended, indeterminate process of perpetual inquiry becomes a way of being. So when one thoughtfully asks "What is design?" what is really meant is, "How can I keep testing my assumptions about architecture and what it means to design?" Or, "How shall I keep questioning how and why I design what I design?"

Swimming in the waters of this type of inquiry will always be hard. For the young designer—looking for his voice, unsure about how to proceed, feeling the pressure of solving a design problem, and wandering away from a theory of design process—inexperience clouds the question. For the experienced designer—confident in her abilities, mature in her practice, technically knowledgeable, and sure-footed—the quick and possibly glib solution arises so quickly, seemingly magical in its effortlessness, that there's no time and certainly no incentive to question it.

Then there's the question of the cognitive quality of designing "by hand" as distinct from designing "digitally" ("computationally" would be more apt, as "digital design" has little to do with fingers). How does the modality of design affect the design outcome? Is an architect exploring a design solution by sketching with pencil and paper favoring a different design outcome than one immersed in a BIM workflow, by virtue of the haptic or cognitive nature of the design process? Does BIM lead to a particular architectural outcome?

Introduction

As a fruitful premise for inquiry (what Socrates in Plato's dialogues calls εικωσ μγθοσ—a "likely story"), let's consider that architecture (as a profession, though perhaps too as a human artifact) has been experiencing an evolving crisis for well over a century. And while we're in Greece, let's also ponder that "architect" is from άρχι and τέκτων: "master builder," or chief craftsman. While some architects may be capable builders, for a very long time the process of design has been divorced from the direct process of making. To be sure, in Europe some architects serve as *maître d'ouvrage* (master of the work), and their professional function is distinct from design architects. Even in the United States, many architects function as project managers. And as with *maîtres d'ouvrage*, their bailiwick encompasses project objectives, scheduling, sequencing, and budgets; they are not builders or craftsmen *per se*. Perhaps not coincidentally, very few architects come up through the profession with a background in building. For better or worse, ours is a profession rooted in the academy.

Arguably, the Viennese Secession, Franco-Belgian Art Nouveau, the British and American Arts and Crafts Movement, and their contemporary localized counterparts were a reformation against mechanized and industrialized fabrication methods coming online over a century ago. (Ironically, nowadays of course one can order Arts and Crafts furniture online, made in a factory overseas and delivered with two-day free shipping. I have no objections to such a convenience, but it does reduce an architectural and artistic movement to a mere style or fetish.) Mechanization has so pervaded our social expression of work that the handcrafted has lost the moral superiority assigned to it by the Arts and Crafts Movement, and is now commodified or fetishized. A century ago windows were produced by hand like custom millwork; now they are mass produced—and with good reason, too, as modern windows assembled with modern materials and manufacturing vastly outperform their historical counterparts.

So on the one hand we have master builders who do not build, and on the other we have building processes that are farther and farther removed from craft (Figure 1.1). In a philosophical context, it may not be a problem that architects do not build anything; it may merely be a needless obsession with an archaic etymology that would suggest that as a profession we should be builders. I for one am not trained in the act of building, nor do I have the urge to exercise it. Except that as the distance from design to execution lengthens, the constructibility of the design may suffer. Moreover, design can be instructed by construction. An architectural detail may be intricately drawn, but what if it cannot be achieved due to the dimensional tolerances required, or if the sequencing of its components would be impossible?

If anything, the abstract nature of architectural design processes only contributes to this gap between the design idea and its physical manifestation. The more abstract the design artifact, the greater the gap. The architect loves the hand-drawn line in part *because* it is so abstract: bearing almost no intrinsic information, an entire story may be inferred from a few accidental details. Is it perfectly straight (a firm decision has been made) or wavering (it describes a vague impulse, or perhaps a natural feature)? Is it ink (confident, authoritative), or soft pencil (tentative, or evocative)? Is it drawn on vellum (final) or trace (exploratory), or on a scrap of napkin (extemporaneous)? Note that all these

FIGURE 1.1 Automated construction of an architectural wall. If the craft isn't in the assembly in the field, where does it lie? In the programming of the automation?

Image courtesy Construction Robotics.

meanings are subjective: they are supplied by the observer, using certain cultural visual cues as a context for assembling a narrative out of a mere line drawn between two points. In other words, the observer infers the meaning (Figure 1.2).

By training moreover, for many architects and designers drawing is much more than merely a means of clearly communicating a comprehensive idea. The act of drawing itself is a cognitive process, an act of uncovering, an exploration. Just as the traveler may not fully see the building he is drawing until he actually draws it, so the architect may not fully realize a design idea *except by drawing it.*

Now consider a BIM assembly. With contemporary BIM-authoring software, it can of course readily be rendered in a hard line; in a sketch style with variable parameters to control wobble, overstrike, and so on; as a cartoon color rendering with graphic qualities reminiscent of Francis D.K. Ching; as a white rendering almost indistinguishable from a museum-board model; as a photo-realistic rendering with depth of field, blur, and complex lighting; and so on (Figure 1.3).

I assert that the modality of a BIM rendering, unlike that of the hand drawing, is a function of the communication of the completed design thought. As typically used, BIM is not as a rule an exploratory device. It may be that this fact contributes to experienced designers' contending that BIM is not a design tool, but only suitable to the refinement, coordination, or documentation of a

FIGURE 1.2 These travel sketches communicate as much with what they omit as by what is explicit. Moreover, the architectural elements of the drawing require that the user interpret the intended representation.

design derived by other means (Figure 1.4). This is a serious error, due perhaps to judging digital processes by analog standards and analog experiences. For the paradigm of the line is not the appropriate one for BIM. Rather, BIM inhabits the world of data, whether abstract or geometric, and should therefore be evaluated performatively and formally, rather than graphically.

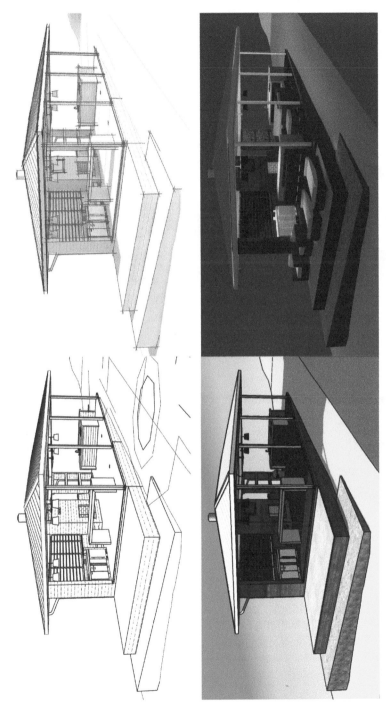

FIGURE 1.3 A series of renderings of the same BIM assembly, illustrating just some of the variety of rendering styles available when rendering in BIM.

5

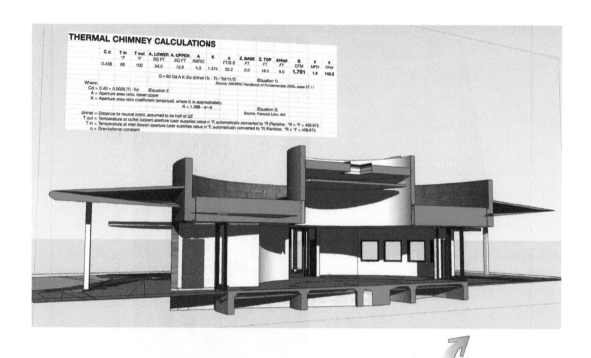

THERMAL CHIMNEY CALCULATIONS

Cd	T in °F	T out °F	A, LOWER SQ FT	A, UPPER SQ FT	A RATIO	K	g FT/S	Z, BASE FT	Z, TOP FT	ΔHnpl FT	Q CFM	v MPH	v FPM
0.438	85	100	54.0	12.6	4.3	1.374	32.2	0.0	18.0	9.0	**1,791**	1.6	149.2

$$Q = 60\ Cd\ A\ K\ (2g\ \Delta Hnpl\ (T_0 - T_i)\ /\ Tol)^{1/2}$$ (Equation 1)
Source: ASHRAE Handbook of Fundamentals 2005, page 27.11

Where:
$Cd = 0.40 + 0.0025\ (T_i - Tol)$ (Equation 2)
A = Aperture area ratio, lower:upper
K = Aperture area ratio coefficient (empirical), where K is approximately:
$K = 1.388 - e^{-A}$ (Equation 2)
Source: François Lévy, AIA

ΔHnpl = Distance to neutral point, assumed to be half of ΔZ
T out = Temperature at outlet (upper) aperture (user supplies value n °F, automatically converted to °R (Rankine; °R = °F + 459.67))
T in = Temperature at inlet (lower) aperture (user supplies value in °F, automatically converted to °R (Rankine; °R = °F + 459.67))
g = Gravitational constant

Wind-Driven Cross Ventilation Calculation

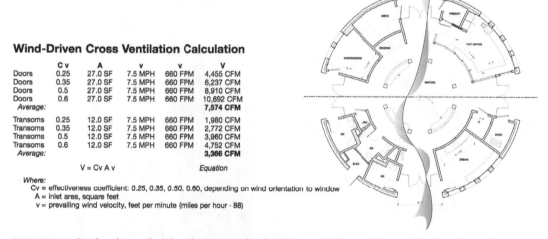

	Cv	A	v	v	V
Doors	0.25	27.0 SF	7.5 MPH	660 FPM	4,455 CFM
Doors	0.35	27.0 SF	7.5 MPH	660 FPM	6,237 CFM
Doors	0.5	27.0 SF	7.5 MPH	660 FPM	8,910 CFM
Doors	0.6	27.0 SF	7.5 MPH	660 FPM	10,692 CFM
Average:					**7,574 CFM**
Transoms	0.25	12.0 SF	7.5 MPH	660 FPM	1,980 CFM
Transoms	0.35	12.0 SF	7.5 MPH	660 FPM	2,772 CFM
Transoms	0.5	12.0 SF	7.5 MPH	660 FPM	3,960 CFM
Transoms	0.6	12.0 SF	7.5 MPH	660 FPM	4,752 CFM
Average:					**3,366 CFM**

$$V = Cv\ A\ v$$ Equation

Where:
Cv = effectiveness coefficient: 0.25, 0.35, 0.50, 0.60, depending on wind orientation to window
A = inlet area, square feet
v = prevailing wind velocity, feet per minute (miles per hour · 88)

FIGURE 1.4 Design investigation in BIM. A single BIM model is used to evaluate a host of performance-based design decisions. Capital Area Rural Transportation System (CARTS) East-side Bus Plaza project design by McCann Adams Studio and Jackson McElhaney Architects; energy and sustainability analysis by the author.

What's Wrong with BIM?

The infamous 2004 NIST study, which "conservatively" identified an estimated $5.3 billion cost to designers and builders in the capital facilities industry in the United States for 2002 alone, helped set the stage for adoption of BIM in construction. The push for adoption was largely led by large-scale construction companies, building owners, and facilities managers. The latter stakeholders especially saw the benefits of the BIM artifact (the building information model), as a tool to potentially more efficiently manage building operations. Contractors were perhaps more sensitive to the possibilities for error reduction in a data-rich 3D building model federated from submodels contributed by the various design disciplines (architecture and civil, structural, and mechanical engineering), but contractors tended to completely rebuild the building information model in-house rather than simply reuse the federated design model. This astonishing apparent inefficiency flies in the face of the collaborative spirit of BIM and has been justified by contractors' differing set of operational parameters. For example, sequencing concerns might suggest that concrete be modeled in discrete divisions based on the maximum concrete volume per pour (Figure 1.5).

Architects, on the other hand, were often reluctant to adopt BIM for a variety of reasons. BIM seemed to expand the architect's services and deliverables with no corresponding increase in fee. BIM required new software,

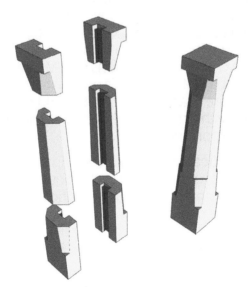

FIGURE 1.5 Two BIM models of architectural concrete components of a project, in this case a cast stone column. The instance at right is modeled as the architect would, in terms of the desired final geometry. The exploded view at left illustrates the cast stone clad elements segregated into individual castings, as the contractor and fabricator would consider it.

hardware, and training—again with no correlation in remuneratioin. More-over, the claim of increased efficiency was met with some skepticism. BIM at its worst is just another file format requirement, and one with high overhead costs. In short, BIM was seen in many cases as a benefit to building owners and contractors at the expense of architects.

Missed Opportunities

And this may be true if in fact the sole or primary objective of BIM was "better, faster, stronger" computer aided design and drafting (CADD, commonly short-ened to CAD. One might rightly wonder whether it's the "design" or the "draft-ing" that got dropped). But to see BIM as CAD+ is frankly shortsighted and misses important and fundamental changes in design approaches enabled by BIM.

BIM [Re]defined

There has already been quite a lot written on the nature of BIM; anything more than a brief definition here might be considered superfluous. Moreover, intentionally or not, definitions tend to be self-serving, advancing the agenda of the author or promulgating a particular view. Nevertheless, it's important to the context of a discussion specifically about BIM for design to consider the following:

▫ **BIM is a social construct** at least as much as it is a technology. For many, underscoring that "BIM is not a technology" actually means that BIM is not a particular, proprietary technology (i.e., Revit). To suggest that BIM is not tech-nological could not be farther from the truth. Moreover, acknowledging the social aspect of BIM is crucial to discussions of BIM's interoperability. That is, one must consider that a BIM workflow is one that allows multiple authors and stakeholders to share graphical (geometry) and tabular (numerical data) project information. Furthermore, BIM is not an island, and it can accept and transmit (import and export) non-BIM data.

▫ **BIM has cognitive implications** for the participant. BIM requires designers and project stakeholders to think differently about the processes of designing, coordination, collaboration, and verification. The relationship bet-ween tool and user is not one-directional; the chosen design tool influences that design outcomes are harder, which are easier, and which are virtually impossible. Our tools influence us (see Chapter 3).

▫ **BIM is data driven.** The BIM file is a comprehensive database of information regarding building components and activities, and boundaries. BIM objects are data rich. For example, a wall contains geometric information (e.g., length, height, thickness, location, surface area, volume, etc.). It is also contextual, able to accept a penetration like a door, window, or louvered vent, and can be tagged with data identifying it as load bearing, with a particular fire rating, STC (sound transmission coefficient), R-value, density, cost per given unit, or any user-defined information desired. This is critical, not merely because it happens to be a historical feature of BIM, but because the inherent data of **BIM gives the designer opportunities to make richer design decisions.**

To summarize: BIM is an architectural digital environment and work process in which data-rich 3- and potentially 4- and 5D building models, composed of contextual building objects, generate dynamically linked graphical and tabular views.

Leveraging BIM Workflows in the Design and Delivery of Complex Projects
Richard Garber, AIA GRO Architects, PLLC, New York, NY, USA

Introduction
GRO Architects is a multidisciplinary architectural office working on projects of varying scales from interiors to planning proposals (Figure 1.6). Over the past decade, we have increasingly utilized technology to realize projects, initially through digital fabrication and ultimately with BIM as projects have grown in size and complexity. Our use of these technologies has expanded beyond design, document execution, and fabrication to the development of a collaborative process for building delivery. To accomplish this, we have become interested in the design of a *workflow* that encompasses as much project scope as possible.

By shifting to a workflow process, as architects we not only control how our work integrates with others on the design and construction team but are also able to expand the territory within which our profession has traditionally operated. Namely, the workflow process moves architectural production from primarily preconstruction phases to ones that directly engage the physical matter of building. It is useful to note that such a tradition of architects working remotely was established by Leon Batista Alberti and others following a period when the architect was intimately involved in building activities on a project site. As BIM continues to impact design practice, both in terms of *novelty* and *efficiency*, it is no coincidence that new modes of production are being likened to a time when architects were known as master builders, such as Filippo Brunelleschi.

Workflow
In a contemporary context, one cannot help but compare a workflow process for architectural design and construction with those that revolutionized business practice some 25 years ago, contemporaneously with 3D modeling

FIGURE 1.6 Harrison Mixed-Use Transit Oriented Development, Harrison, New Jersey. GRO Architects is using BIM in the early design stages of large-scale planning projects. By linking variables like program, assigned by material; number of stories; and metrics for unit and parking count, our practice is exploring way to scale BIM technology to urban plans.

Image courtesy GRO Architects.

software's initial broad foray into our profession. Referred to as business process reengineering (BPR), these processes relied heavily on information technology (IT) to lessen the importance of individual tasks and refocus the flow of work on the achievement of value. Interestingly, a term being used both in the architectural profession and in business and enterprise development is that of "continuous improvement," defined as the cumulative addition of both breakthrough and continuous enhancements to a product or process. By allowing for more design iteration and integration during preconstruction activities, BIM has allowed architects to expand the territory within which they operate while allowing for better buildings.

Unlike methods of production in the twentieth century, which privileged the linear and rote repetition of tasks by relatively unskilled workers, these BIM-enabled improvement flows can be discontinuous. Following the work of W.E. Demming and others, an integrated design and construction team can bring differing approaches covering separate but related areas of building. These are merged and refined within a single or federated digital model shared across a large team responsible for design and construction. What is at stake is not the architectural design process becoming overly codified, but rather its being technologically and technically rationalized to be both novel and efficient—two sometimes oppositional goals in architectural practice.

To illustrate a varied design process utilizing digital tools, the case study that follows utilizes a workflow that, through BIM, engages a variety of stakeholders and team members in the actualization of projects of different scope and scale.

Case Study: Harrison Mixed-Use, Transit-Oriented Development

GRO is designing a mixed-use development between the PATH Station and Red Bull Arena, opened in 2010, in Harrison, New Jersey, that will expand retail, hospitality, and entertainment opportunities and brings residential, office, and structured parking programs to a commuter hub some 20 minutes from Lower Manhattan (Figure 1.7). Bound to the south where the Passaic River flows to Newark Bay is a major nexus of railway (Amtrak, NJTransit, PATH) and roadway (Interstate 280, NJ Turnpike) infrastructures; the site, a portion of a 250-acre (101.1 ha) former industrial waterfront area has been declared an area in need of redevelopment. Since 2012, the municipality has intended to see its

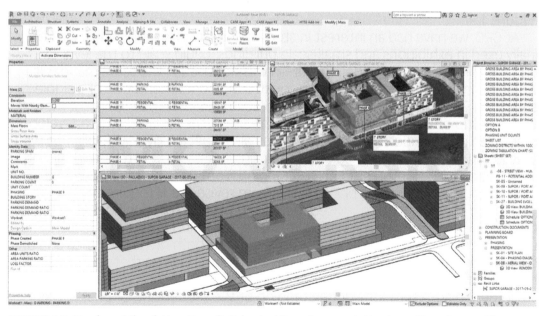

FIGURE 1.7 Harrison Mixed-Use, Transit Oriented Development, Harrison, New Jersey. The process of manipulating the BIM based on real-time input allowed the team to see metrics change automatically. Through this process, GRO was able to forecast better design options that remain financially feasible.

Image courtesy GRO Architects.

transformation into a walkable and transit-oriented development. The vision for the area, elaborated by Susan Gruel of Heyer Gruel & Associates, the municipality's community planning consultant, is to "create a vibrant mixed-use, transit-oriented, pedestrian-scale development that will make Harrison a regional destination for years to come."

For GRO's plan, a series of 10 phases have been imagined to bring 1.3 million square feet (120,774 m²) of development as well as 3,500 new parking spaces to the commuter hub, over 2,200 of which will be unrestricted. Interestingly, the project metrics were driven by parking, with the municipality needing to satisfy the requirements of a subway expansion plan that will increase ridership from 7,300 to 13,000 between 2012 and 2022, between Newark, New Jersey (the last stop immediately west of the project), Jersey City, and finally New York City to the east. The design team has imagined a dynamic mix of pedestrian-friendly programs and uses that will activate the area bound by the PATH station to the west and the arena to the east (Figure 1.8).

Following the construction of a new looping roadway, a series of phased buildings are proposed. Key elements of the plan include a retail base under many of the buildings for a total of 166,800 square feet (15,496 m²) of retail. This brings a walkable aspect to the proposed plan that will link the new station with the arena by a 60'0" (18.3 m) wide dedicated pedestrian street (Figure 1.9).

At GRO, we have had an interest in studying how digital tools, which we originally used in exhibitions and small-scale buildings, could scale to the level of urban planning. While a modeling system was not used in the same manner it would be in the development of, say, construction documentation of a single structure, BIM was heavily utilized to understand real-time development metrics of the group of structures imagined for the site as they related to a redevelopment plan being undertaken by the municipality. Specifically, BIM's ability to parametrically update data ensured that the design team was able to share current information with all interested parties ranging from the municipality to investors. Changes to the overall plan ranging from revised radii requirements in the plotting of the new road to revised metes and bounds for specific sites within the plan were accounted for in real time. By establishing typical loss factors and unit sizes for the residential and parking programs, both gross floor area and unit counts were maintained. Shadow studies were developed so that appropriate heights for buildings could be proposed and incorporated into a revised redevelopment plan. A temporal understanding of the sequencing of phases was understood through the BIM as well.

The model was also linked and shared via CSV-format data to populate a development term sheet used to establish project worth to investors, and a running preliminary cost estimate for the design team. As a result, a precise

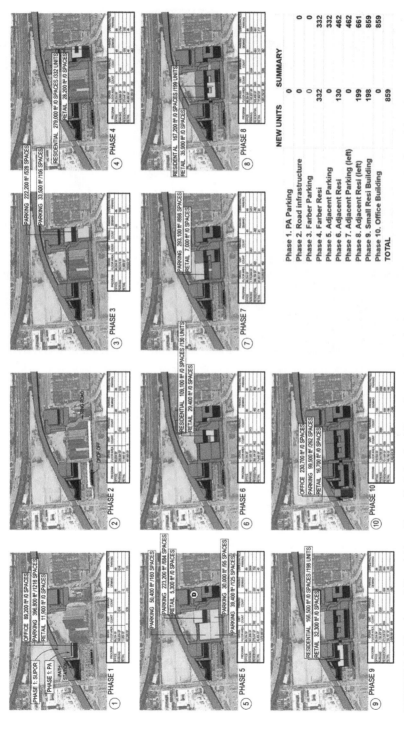

FIGURE 1.8 Harrison Mixed-Use, Transit-Oriented Development, Harrison, New Jersey. GRO's BIM for this urban planning project included temporal phasing data. This data was critical in illustrating to the municipality that parking demand would be met while still demonstrating the project's financial viability, which was of high importance to the development group.

Image courtesy GRO Architects.

FIGURE 1.9 Harrison Mixed-Use, Transit-Oriented Development, Harrison, New Jersey. A 60'0" wide dedicated pedestrian corridor that links the Harrison PATH Station to the Red Bull Arena is a critical component to the project. The walkway, which is programmed with retail along its entire expanse, will ensure that both commuters and soccer fans will have retail and hospitality options to explore while spending time in Harrison.

Image courtesy GRO Architects.

financial dossier was assembled so that project work and cost per phase could be established.

One of the most remarkable things about this process was how BIM allowed an expanded team to come together and make decisions to drive the direction of the project. While the architects remained the designers and purveyors of the data, the data was parsed and translated to allow the team to expand beyond designers and engineering consultants to include planners, attorneys, financial consultants, developer's representatives, traffic experts, and municipal officers—all speaking a related, if not common, language contained within BIM.

While potentially increasing the architect's scope and role in project design and delivery, the building information model, as precise data, can be parsed in a variety of ways to increase the knowledge of stakeholders. While the intent is not to adopt a "design by committee" schema—the architect should always retain an authorial role—the notion of being more inclusive in the design workflow, especially during preconstruction activities, can lead to more effective communication and a better-informed team during actual building delivery.

BIM in Academia: How BIM Is Taught

As one might expect, there exist varied approaches to the integration of building information modeling in the professional pedagogy. These methods lie on a spectrum from a full acknowledgment and teaching of BIM to a tacit implication that BIM is "merely a tool" and need not be part of the curriculum. In some architecture schools, students are given technical instruction in BIM as a distinct curricular subject, much as they might learn visual communication, statics, or environmental controls. In other academic programs, BIM is considered just another kind of software, not explicitly addressed in the formal curriculum at all, and students are expected to pick it up along the way, just as they might learn Photoshop from YouTube videos. It's been my anecdotal experience that the more a school considers itself a mainstay of high design, the more BIM is seen as "just a tool" and the less it is considered to be a legitimate academic endeavor. Naturally, even in "design-oriented" programs one will find academics with progressive views on BIM as a design environment, just as one may encounter Luddites in more technically oriented programs.

Karen Kensek, an assistant professor at the University of Southern California School of Architecture, teaches computer applications for architecture, is on the Facade Tectonics Institute steering committee, and with her colleague Douglas Noble organizes the annual USC BIM Conference. She relates that, currently, USC has a dual approach to introducing both graduate and undergraduate students to BIM in the architectural curriculum—offering instruction in both required and elective courses. First, BIM is incorporated into the second semester of the required professional practice course, with an emphasis on the use of drawings to communicate between the various stakeholders in the design and construction process. The comprehensive projects the students develop also incorporate mechanical and structural components while highlighting the importance of coordination within design and documentation drawings. Guest speakers from architecture, construction, and fabrication firms also speak to the class about innovative uses of BIM in the industry.

In the elective undergraduate BIM class, there is typically a secondary theme that changes from year to year; in the past it has been the use of BIM with analysis software, specifically for sustainable design, but for collaboration as well. Students in this class are often architecture students, but also several are from the geodesign major. The graduate version of the class includes a strong BIM visual programming (or graphical scripting) element, where students learn how to customize software and create new tools. This class also attracts an academically more diverse group of students, from architecture, building science, and engineering programs. Interested students are encouraged to take the BIM graduate course in construction management as it covers a very different set of issues.

The USC program offers elective courses in BIM or BIM-related topics at both the undergraduate and graduate level, including Advanced Computation, Advanced Fabrication, Architectural Technology, Computer Applications in Architecture, Descriptive and Computational Architectural Geometry, Digital Tools in Architecture, Media for Landscape Architecture: 3D Design, and Theories of Computer Technology.

In addition to coursework, graduate students have the opportunity to focus on BIM for their thesis projects. Recent topics have included interoperability between BIM and energy software, BIM and virtual reality, and potential uses of BIM in heritage conservation. As with the advent of CAD and then 3D modeling in the past, there is a progression in the curriculum where more fundamental ideas are incorporated into other classes, and the "BIM" courses evolve to focus on more advanced and innovative topics (see Figure 1.10).

In almost any academic environment, there is a tension between students' concern with learning skills with direct employment applications, potentially in opposition to—and at times at the expense of—gaining a deeper understanding of the appropriate use of technology. Kensek acknowledges that there is a clear desire by students to learn specific software skills for their résumés. That does not necessarily sacrifice deeper thinking, however. Ideally, a teaching approach is designed for both of these tendencies to build on each other. Her homework assignments are very much software based, and yet are grounded in concepts she wants her students to learn, as well as augmented by appropriate readings. For example, one topic she stresses is the use of data in the building model and how it can or cannot be transferred to other software programs; while students are using the software and learning commands they think are of practical value, they learn processes through successes and failures that are even more important in the long term. Sometimes students learn things that they may not think of as BIM or even valuable; one semester Kensek spent a couple weeks of C# programming with the expectation that her past coding experience is applicable to student learning.

According to Kensek, students who attend the USC BIM Conference are truly amazed that topics they have learned in class from their professors and guest lecturers are not mere academic exercises but have real-world applications. They recognize that BIM is bigger and more exciting than they ever thought,

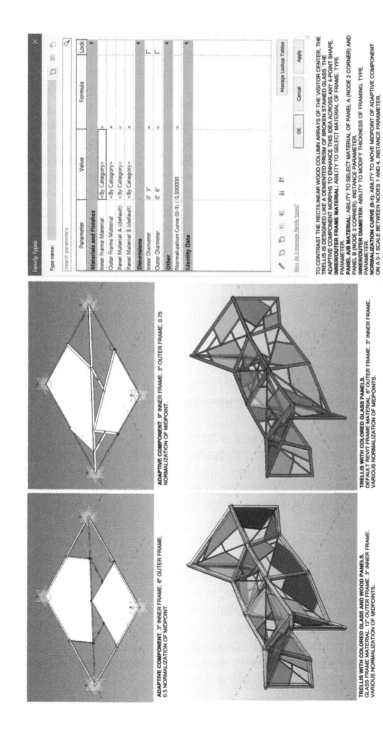

ADAPTIVE COMPONENT. 3" INNER FRAME. 8" OUTER FRAME.
0.5 NORMALIZATION OF MIDPOINT.

ADAPTIVE COMPONENT. 9" INNER FRAME. 3" OUTER FRAME. 0.75
NORMALIZATION OF MIDPOINT.

TRELLIS WITH COLORED GLASS AND WOOD PANELS.
GLASS FRAME MATERIAL. 12" OUTER FRAME. 3" INNER FRAME.
VARIOUS NORMALIZATION OF MIDPOINTS.

TRELLIS WITH COLORED GLASS PANELS.
DEFAULT REVIT FRAME MATERIAL. 6" OUTER FRAME. 3" INNER FRAME.
VARIOUS NORMALIZATION OF MIDPOINTS.

TO CONTRAST THE RECTILINEAR WOOD COLUMN ARRAYS OF THE VISITOR CENTER, THE TRELLIS IS DESIGNED LIKE A DEMENTED PRISM OF BROKEN STAINED GLASS. THE ADAPTIVE COMPONENT MORPHS TO ENHANCE THIS IDEA ACROSS ANY 4-POINT SHAPE.
INNER/OUTER FRAME MATERIAL: ABILITY TO SELECT MATERIAL OF FRAME. TYPE PARAMETER.
PANEL A/B MATERIAL: ABILITY TO SELECT MATERIAL OF PANEL A (NODE 2 CORNER) AND PANEL B (NODE 3 CORNER). INSTANCE PARAMETER.
INNER/OUTER DIAMETER: ABILITY TO MODIFY THICKNESS OF FRAMING. TYPE PARAMETER.
NORMALIZATION CURVE (0-1): ABILITY TO MOVE MIDPOINT OF ADAPTIVE COMPONENT ON A 0-1 SCALE BETWEEN NODES 1 AND 4. INSTANCE PARAMETER.

FIGURE 1.10 An example of graphical scripting, generating a 3D model from a series of inputs and algorithmic operations.

Image credit: Noah Cherner, USC School of Architecture student.

and rather than being one piece of software or one narrow topic, it is a broad field that covers a profuse area of design, construction, and even facilities management. Students see that expanse and want to be part of it.

Students seem very engaged in graphical scripting, far more so than most practicing architects (older professionals may think that Grasshopper is a passé cocktail rather than a popular graphical scripting module for Rhino, a 3D surface modeler). While visual programming may be the next wave in design technology that younger designers are eager to embrace, it may be a niche design process with limited relevance in the prosaic world of kitchen remodels, health care projects, K–12 schools, and building permits. For Kensek, programming and scripting are important, as they allow for another type of designer to contribute to the design process. Moreover, coding is freedom: it allows those who understand it to customize their digital world and not be trapped by tools a software developer decided to provide.

In her graduate BIM course, Kensek's current approach is to assign relatively simple exercises that are not discouraging or frustrating. One assignment, for example, was to change the size of an opening based on the sun's location. She then gives an open-ended team project for student groups to explore their own interests. Sometimes the student projects are exciting or surprising; one year, a team of students demonstrated using Alexa to have their 3D model respond to voice commands to open and shut shading devices, a wholly unexpected approach. A few students conclude that coding isn't for them, and those are balanced by a few who have found a new career option that they previously did not even know existed.

Looking forward, Kensek sees several emerging or recently emerged technologies that can fit under a "big tent" definition of BIM: big data, simulation, additive manufacturing (3D printing) and rapid prototyping, graphical scripting, data-driven design, and the use of drones, robotic construction, and virtual and augmented reality (Figures 1.11 and 1.12). Kensek has published on another emerging technology: the integration of environmental sensors with BIM, using Arduino or comparable devices to program the built environment. This simple, mono-chip microcomputer executes programs created in the Processing programming language. It can be adapted as a software interface, a robotic control system, a data recorder in conjunction with an array of available sensor types, for kinetically responsive art installations, as well as for other applications. In spite of an expanding ecosystem of technology in architectural practice, Kensek sees more optimism that technology can be appropriately applied, and that her school and others are exploring exciting new possibilities. One has only to look in on architecture studios for inspiration!

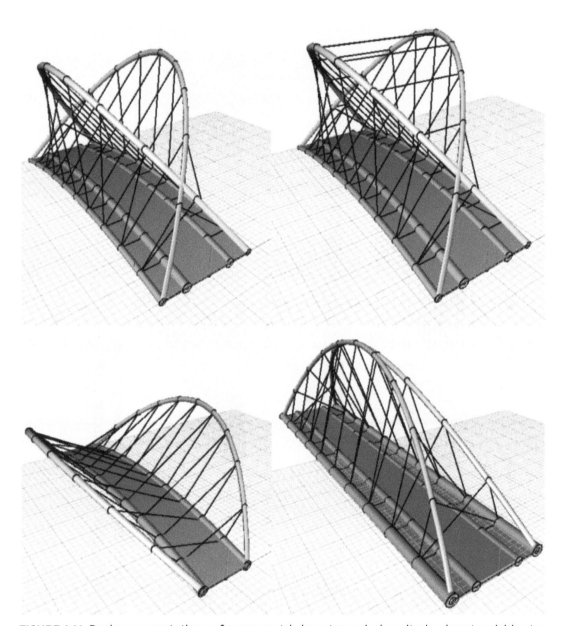

FIGURE 1.11 Design permutations of a parametric bow truss design altering input variables to achieve variation in modeling outcome.

Image credit: Noah Cherner, USC School of Architecture student.

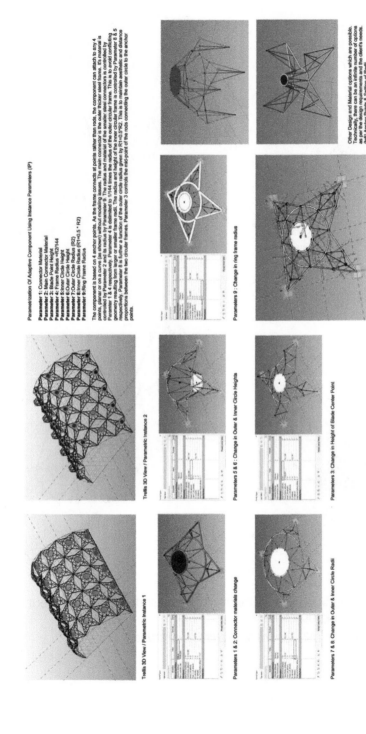

FIGURE 1.12 A computational BIM conceptual modeling exercise.

Image credit: Kushnav Roy, USC School of Architecture student.

Case Study: Guadalupe Parking Garage Green Wall Pilot Project

Danelle Briscoe, Assistant Professor in Architecture, The University of Texas at Austin School of Architecture, Austin, TX, USA

This proposal (with co-primary investigator Mark Simmons and former UTSOA dean Fritz Steiner) for a green wall comprising plants either supported on a trellis structure ("green façade") or rooted in growing media attached to the wall itself (a "living wall" similar to a prototype designed and constructed on campus) has environmental benefit potential for buildings and structural partition walls. Green walls can be both beautiful and functional. They can be an effective air purifying system: the wall is a natural air filter, removing particulate matter, O_3, volatile organic compounds, and CO_2 from the air as it passes through or across the wall. Similarly, a green wall can cool building surfaces and interior space and even reduce ambient air temperature around the building—helping to mitigate the urban heat-island effect. Other benefits include storm water mitigation (through transpiration and soil infiltration) and habitat for beneficial fauna including pollinators (hummingbirds, butterflies), songbirds, and raptors (owls, hawks).

However, the design of extensive green walls in a hot, dry climate can pose some challenges, and appropriate systems and plants species have been poorly explored. Previous research conducted by Simmons and Briscoe on suitability of plants for green (vegetated) roofs and green walls has indicated that there are suites of plant species, tolerant of high root temperatures and limited water availability, appropriate for this application, although this has yet to be extensively tested for green walls in this subtropical climate.

The critical factors in determining a structural proposal are soil volume, existing building right-of-way, and the desire for component variability to act as a trellis, container, and bio-habitat. As a means to growing plants at multiple levels of the garage, the project proposes the fabrication of "trough-like" soil containers to sit behind the existing concrete spandrel, reducing standard parking spaces along the west side of the building to compact spaces. The irrigation line and drainage will be incorporated into this system. This container will allow greater soil volume in the green wall, and is also self-shaded from the intensity of the west-facing sun. The proposed geometry of the trellis and living system will allow for the integration of detailed habitats, such as for birds or bats.

Advanced 3D fabrication. 3D printed cells in varying colors correspond to plant types in the BIM model and optimized pattern-making arrangement (Figure 1.13); BIM is integral to the design/fabrication process in that the initial modular studies could very easily translate to STL files for 3D printing. Color-coded 3D prints express the plant pattern. Advanced data monitoring for a year of four cells on the wall would allow the wall to interactively report its

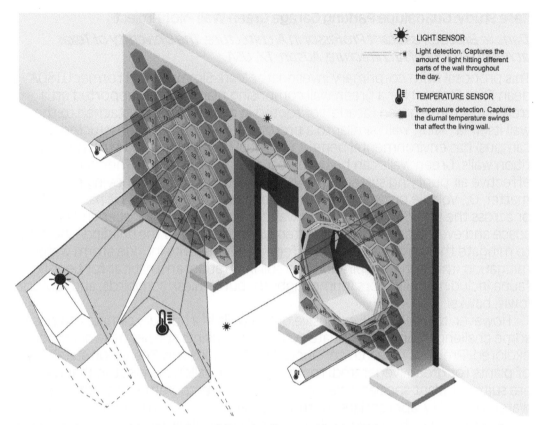

LIGHT SENSOR

Light detection. Captures the amount of light hitting different parts of the wall throughout the day.

TEMPERATURE SENSOR

Temperature detection. Captures the diurnal temperature swings that affect the living wall.

FIGURE 1.13 Axonometric rendering of the planting, and light and temperature sensor of a BIM modeled green wall prototype installed at the University of Texas at Austin School of Architecture.

Image courtesy of Danelle Briscoe.

full physical state through a QR code and the Smart Water system established by UT facilities maintenance director for water, Marcus Hogue. A novel approach to BIM modeling is achieved by through his software to detect the activity of selected cells, primarily through monitoring water distribution and temperature.

Advanced coordination. Beyond merely improving documentation and coordination, BIM assisted in the exchange among stakeholders regarding the depth of the planter component, one of the biggest determining factors (Figure 1.14). Several competing agendas had to be resolved: the wall is near a power line on San Jacinto Street that would be cost-prohibitive to bury; on the other hand, ecologists and landscape designers preferred as much soil as

FIGURE 1.14 The completed and operational green wall prototype on campus at the UT Austin School of Architecture.

Photo credit: Whit Preston Photography.

possible (primarily for root temperature). By working with the angle of inclination (i.e., skewed geometry) of the component, a self-shading cell was designed that is estimated to decrease the root temperature by 30° F (17° C) on a 100° F (38° C) day, based on past experience with cacti.

Novel pattern making. Particular design opportunities are to be found through scheduling and data-rich "material" capabilities in BIM. Each cell is assigned a given color and corresponding plant species (and all its attributes specified by Lady Bird Johnson Wildflower Center ecologists) in Revit's Material Editor. Plant parameters are embedded within each type's Properties menu, which can then be scheduled as a material take-off quantity from each generated pattern, as if it were a sum of building material. By having each plant type read as a single, abstract color, the information model allows for greater legibility of the patterns, reducing memory usage, yet retains all the information from the plant data sheet (Figure 1.15). The pairing of hexagons begins to strategize a nested solution for developing a reduction in file size and reducing the computational generation time of each potential pattern. Managing processing and rendering time is critical for increasing interoperability solutions between the different components of the project. In order to establish a construction budget, plant types and quantities must be accurately known, and they influence factors such as water use and soil hardiness.

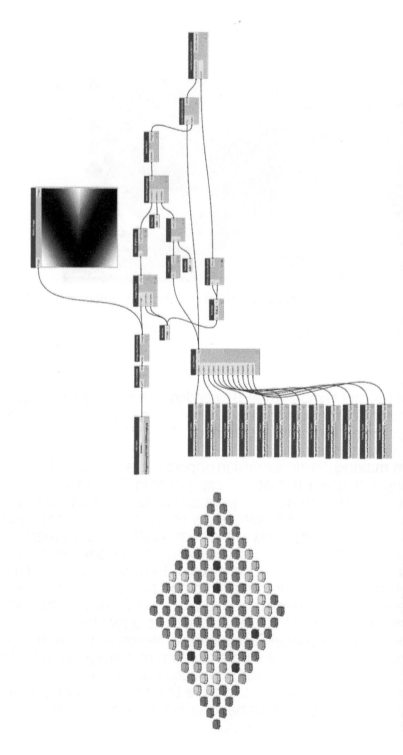

FIGURE 1.15 A graphical script used to generate color-coded planter cells. Gray blocks bearing Dynamo scripts are arranged in a visual flow chart; "wires" show the flow of data and operations left to right. The automated model output can be quickly varied and iterated by changing input variables.

Image courtesy of Danelle Briscoe.

Novel design workflow. We experimented with Revit family files containing Rich Photographic Content (RPC) for each plant, in an effort to assist in the visualization of the pattern generation and to produce renderings of each pattern iteration. In effect, 2D and 3D views were able to display plant entourage images using simple line drawings as placeholders. In pursuit of data-to-vector relationships, some placeholders were found to "misbehave" by inconsistently changing their orientation. When rendering a 3D view, the photo-realistic plant entourage was displayed in the rendered image, but proved to be item-consuming to calculate and render and the quality of the renderings could suffer. A possible alternative that could reduce data redundancy per component would be to create more populous nested components, each acting as a single agent in the pattern generation.

The algorithm to create patterns of planters assigned each distinct hexagonal component type to a corresponding pixel's grayscale value of a bitmap. This methodology stands apart from (what has become) a very common practice in visual programming as each pattern results in a material take-off schedule for ecological relationships or other aspects of feasibility testing. For example, in one bitmap test pattern, the black-to-white gradient application was reversed, thereby changing the aesthetics of the pattern due to plant color allocation. Such a simple shift of correspondences in the bitmap dramatically influenced both the cost of the tested scheme and the ratio of Lepidoptera (butterfly) linkages due to plant combinations created. In this particular case, the quantity of sideoats grama grass doubled, with both cost and performance implications as ecological optimization is linked to plant distribution in the visual pattern.

Species selection. Plant selection is based on a number of factors: known survivability on green roofs or pots, broad ecological niche (e.g., wet or dry soils) and habitat value. Those faunal species that can be encouraged by a green wall are easily found in the urban environment or can be induced to use food sources or constructed habitat. These include the anole lizards, Mexican free-tail bat, numerous butterfly species, and hummingbirds. A BIM has been modeled to parametrically control and schedule planting options as design schemes of the selected species (Figure 1.16). A partial version of one of the planting plans will be utilized in this pilot. For the intent of a design feedback loop, specific information on plant relationships can be flagged from the pilot as ones that enhance and help establish the bio-habitats for the full install. This then will be further explored and research within the simulation of the BIM model.

FIGURE 1.16 A detail of the campus prototype wall, showing the integration of a bird shelter in one of the hexagonal planter cells.

Photo credit: Whit Preston Photography.

BIM milestones. This project has established several procedural landmarks:

- Exploration of the potential of graphical scripting (Dynamo in this case) to handle visual programming for design iteration at the scale of landscape and building.

- Emphasis on BIM data process, not merely BIM drawings or modeling process, representing a shift away from treating BIM as merely a CAD documentation tool.

- Use of Revit/Dynamo as an ecological and landscape design tool with collaborative databases between multiple disciplines; more specifically, the deployment of BIM to support design, scheduling, and future tracking of ecological behavior through a 4D and 5D platform like Navisworks.

- Further insights in BIM design process refinement and streamlining. Current methodology requires at least three to four software applications, and this may be an area of innovation.

◻ Further research will investigate the manner in which components correspond to visual patterns, where beneficial relationships are flagged (analogous to flagging of clash detection instances). For example, two plants with a high ecology rating in proximity could trigger a graphical indication, alerting the designer. In other words, the pattern's optimization is legible.

Conclusion

There is and always has been a natural tension between "architecture" as the thing designed and eventually built, and "architecture" as a practice. We even call our firms, "practices." One is about an external experience, whether objectified as a sculptural object ("I like it as a thing") or experienced as a phenomenological place with particular qualities of spatial organization, light, views, materials, textures, and acoustics. The other is about a generative process that is part invention, part analysis. Even if it were possible to fully disambiguate the two architectures, building and design, it's not evident that that would be for the best.

The experience of architecture as physical artifact is enriched by the perception, understanding, or imagination of the processes that have brought it to life. Kant speaks of the beautiful and the sublime. The former is merely aesthetically attractive; the latter inspires awe and ennobles the viewer by shrinking him before the majesty of the scene. For Kant the sublime can only be found in the domain of nature, which dwarfs human beings with its awful majesty. But I would argue that great architecture (even if modest in scale) can also be sublime in the sense that as we experience it we know, perhaps instinctively or subliminally, that someone gave a great deal of thought, attention, and effort into its making. The care in the designing of a thing increases its value.

For its part, the design process is a mere intellectual or conceptual exercise without an artifact to birth. More pragmatically, the design process is informed and honed by construction. Knowledge of material properties, norms of construction techniques, the sequencing of assemblies, and even the relative costs of building materials are a critical foundation of good design. Moreover, we learn from our mistakes, even (especially) if those can be painful or expensive once executed in the field. I recall drawing details as a young designer fresh out of school, learning by emulating others in the office. But it wasn't until I spent time on job sites that I really understood what I was doing and could meaningfully contribute new solutions to construction detailing problems. The architectural artifact exists in the context of a preexisting reality (site, environment, social milieu) and the realities of construction processes (materials, labor, time, and costs). In order to fit or transform those realities, the designer must understand individual elements and their relationships, often through simulation,

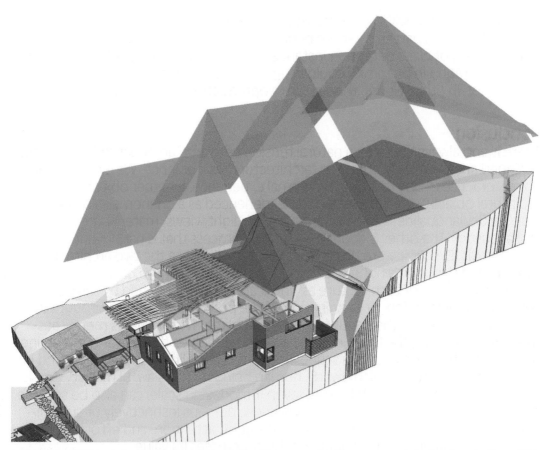

FIGURE 1.17 Site and programmatic investigation are a fertile source of design inspiration; BIM particularly and computational design generally are rich methods of discovery.

experimentation, and trial and error. That understanding is achieved through a process of investigation.

Such a process of investigation is thus fundamental to the design process and to architecture as practice. Nondesigners may labor under the impression that architects are artists, designs springing from their heads fully armed like Athena. Maybe for a few of us that is the case. But in my experience, a design arises out of a process of inquiry into the nature of a site, the needs and means of a client or user, and the realities of construction. BIM offers an opportunity to inquire or investigate in a variety of interdependent modalities: modeling in three dimensions existing and proposed conditions, and analyzing data or information inherent to or attached to that geometry. In some cases BIM gives rise to computational design, simulating the performance of components or assemblies, and/or algorithmically generating responses to variable inputs (Figure 1.17). At the heart of that is investigation.

Chapter 2

BIM Past and Present

with Jeffrey Ouellette *Assoc. AIA,*
Justin Dowhower *AIA, LEED AP, WELL AP and*
Brian P. Skripac *Assoc. AIA, LEED AP BD+C, Vice President, CannonDesign*

Building information modeling (BIM) has gained wide usage in a variety of practices, from large architecture, engineering, and construction (AEC) design-build firms to sole design practitioners—albeit to a lesser degree in smaller firms. In addition to developing a working definition of BIM, this chapter traces the history of BIM from its origins rooted in computer-aided design and drafting (CADD) and its current applications in today's building industry.

A Brief History of BIM

BIM as we know it today has evolved significantly over the past four decades and has now become the de facto standard for documentation, construction, and even certain design/validation workflows in the public and commercial building industry, and increasingly common (while not yet ubiquitous) in small commercial and residential projects. To understand the origins of BIM, we first need to define what it is:

- BIM is a collection of information, workflows, processes, relationships, and communication optimally enabled by digital tools.

- BIM is multidimensional, addressing static and dynamic information throughout the entire life cycle of a project.

- BIM is a comprehensive database of geometric and non-geometric information that can be continually edited and queried.

- BIM is most useful when the information is accessible and interoperable across multiple building industry technologies and workflows.

- BIM is most successful when it is usable and upgradeable over time.

Before BIM, there was the development of CADD, and before that everything was drawn by hand (with the assistance of drafting implements like parallel bars, T-squares, French or flexible curves, technical pens and clutch pencils, mechanical and electric erasers, a huge array of traceable templates, and a variety of lettering tools) to convey instructions for constructing the built environment. Seemingly very different from hand drawing, CADD is in fact cognitively very similar to it. Like its manual predecessor, it too is a two-dimensional workflow, albeit improved in consistency, speed, and accuracy of documentation. Since the 1970s, CADD tools were developed using vectors to define fixed geometry, and these have been adapted for building documentation. While many CADD applications have expanded to include 3D modeling capabilities, those still follow the old paradigm of 2D drafting. CADD still requires manual "assembly" of the building parts, and there is no real syntactical intelligence associated with drawn elements. That is, a pair of parallel lines with an infill is merely the graphical representation of a wall and exhibits no wall-like behavior. Similarly, a heavy-lined rectangle does not have any data associating it with the column it represents, and that therefore limits how it can be computationally structurally analyzed. Moreover, if changes are made to a building design, the user is required to update all CADD drawings more or less manually. Essentially, CADD has replaced the pen and paper with the mouse and computer monitor—both methodologies are nearly equally error prone and tedious. It is also important to recognize that in both cases the delivery of a project relies purely on the quality and completeness of the drawings themselves. The drawings, along with manually written specifications, are the expression of data, the information of how to construct the building (Figure 2.1). Such drawings are subject to wide interpretation, leading to potential errors.

While manual and digital drafting still has a place in design practice (for example, in generating very quick or loose concept sketches or test-fits for site planning exercises), these are inefficient methods for managing the plethora of information and complexity that comprise modern buildings—both from a perspective of time commitment required to produce technical drawings, and the cost associated with correcting human errors. Hence, the advent of BIM authoring tools.

Patterned on software and workflows first utilized by the product manufacturing, aircraft, and automotive industries (known as *product life cycle management* or PLM), BIM is a method of handling complex three-dimensional geometry and associated information in well-structured, semantically described databases. Such geometry may be controlled by parameters—hence known as *"parametric modeling"*—but not all BIM is necessarily parametric. Conservative as it is, the construction industry has slowly evolved and adopted BIM as the preferred technological workflow over the past 20 years. It is important to make the distinction that BIM is not solely about software technologies; rather, it encompasses both digital modeling and the collaborative process for managing project database information between a multitude of users and stakeholders. BIM allows various users to contribute and access information, using it in numerous ways and simultaneously adding/modifying information in an interconnected and relational workflow (Figure 2.2).

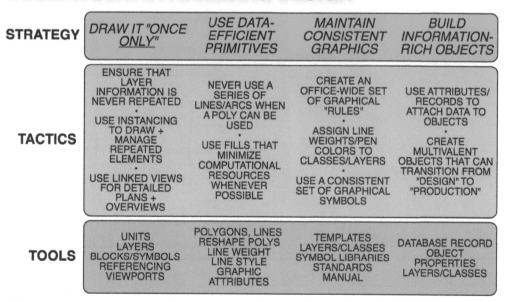

MANUAL DRAFTING GOAL

PRODUCE A CLEAN, CRISP DRAWING EFFICIENTLY

STRATEGY	*MINIMIZE SMUDGING*	*MINIMIZE TOOL CHANGES*	*PRODUCE CONSISTENT LINE WEIGHTS*	*PRODUCE CLEAR NOTATION*
TACTICS	WORK FROM UL TO LR • KEEP ELBOWS + TUMMY OFF DRAWING • LUBRICATE DRAWING + TOOLS • MINIMIZE TOOL CONTACT WITH DRAWING	DRAW ALL GUIDE LINES FIRST • DRAW ARCS TANGENT TO GUIDE LINES • DRAW STRAIGHT LINES AWAY FROM ARCS	EMPHASIZE ENDS OF LINES • ROTATE YOUR PENCIL AS YOU DRAW • USE DIFFERENT LEAD GRADES FOR DIFFERENT LINE WEIGHTS	USE A LETTERING GUIDE • USE A TRIANGLE FOR LETTER VERTICALS • USE A LEROY OR KROY FOR DRAWING TITLES
TOOLS	SPIROLL GROUND RUBBER LIFTING DOTS	COMPASS CIRCLE TEMPLATE GUIDE LINE LEADS PARALLEL BAR TRIANGLE	LEAD POINTER "STABBER" LEAD HOLDER LEADS	LETTERING GUIDE KROY MACHINE/ LEROY SET PARALLEL BAR TRIANGLE

CADD GOAL

COMMUNICATE A BUILDING DESIGN

STRATEGY	*DRAW IT "ONCE ONLY"*	*USE DATA-EFFICIENT PRIMITIVES*	*MAINTAIN CONSISTENT GRAPHICS*	*BUILD INFORMATION-RICH OBJECTS*
TACTICS	ENSURE THAT LAYER INFORMATION IS NEVER REPEATED • USE INSTANCING TO DRAW + MANAGE REPEATED ELEMENTS • USE LINKED VIEWS FOR DETAILED PLANS + OVERVIEWS	NEVER USE A SERIES OF LINES/ARCS WHEN A POLY CAN BE USED • USE FILLS THAT MINIMIZE COMPUTATIONAL RESOURCES WHENEVER POSSIBLE	CREATE AN OFFICE-WIDE SET OF GRAPHICAL "RULES" • ASSIGN LINE WEIGHTS/PEN COLORS TO CLASSES/LAYERS • USE A CONSISTENT SET OF GRAPHICAL SYMBOLS	USE ATTRIBUTES/ RECORDS TO ATTACH DATA TO OBJECTS • CREATE MULTIVALENT OBJECTS THAT CAN TRANSITION FROM "DESIGN" TO "PRODUCTION"
TOOLS	UNITS LAYERS BLOCKS/SYMBOLS REFERENCING VIEWPORTS	POLYGONS, LINES RESHAPE POLYS LINE WEIGHT LINE STYLE GRAPHIC ATTRIBUTES	TEMPLATES LAYERS/CLASSES SYMBOL LIBRARIES STANDARDS MANUAL	DATABASE RECORD OBJECT PROPERTIES LAYERS/CLASSES

FIGURE 2.1 Compare manual drafting processes (above) to CADD "rules" (below). They each have their own distinct cognitive qualities, yet each requires that the user interpret discontinuous two-dimensional drawings to infer a three-dimensional project.

Illustration based on UT Austin class presentation by Robert F. Anderson.

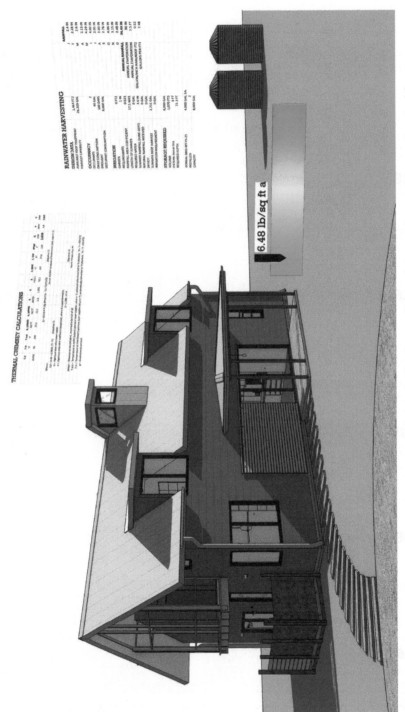

FIGURE 2.2 In BIM, graphical views ("drawings") and data in the form of schedules and reports are extracted from a comprehensive, potentially federated, data-rich building model.

The Right Project for BIM

In its early days, BIM was viewed as a technological workflow that was almost exclusively for large-scale complex construction projects. This was the case for several reasons:

- BIM was (and arguably still is) largely seen as having significant benefits for construction processes first, facilities management and documentation tied for second, and design a distant last, if at all.

- Large projects implied a level of complexity as well as a great deal of repetitive conditions, both of which benefit from a higher degree of intelligent automation.

- Smaller projects tend to involve smaller design teams, where extensive sharing of design data (or drawings) may be far less than for larger design teams. With BIM's emphasis on common or federated models shared by various design disciplines, many smaller firms may have felt that those capabilities weren't relevant to their design and documentation processes.

- In its aspect as a new software technology (even though it's more than that) as well as its inherently greater complexity over CADD, BIM had high development costs. Higher software costs may be easier to be borne by larger firms. Similarly, BIM software tends to be computationally more intensive, requiring more performative hardware. Again, such "seat costs" may be easier to bear for a large firm.

However, as the price of the software tools has decreased, and the sophistication of the technologies have increased, the case is being made for a BIM-fits-all approach to design and construction.

The most recent published AIA Firm Survey Report shows 28% BIM adoption in small firms in 2013 and 2015. Interestingly, a roughly contemporaneous McGraw-Hill survey (which polled broad types of AEC firms, not just architecture practices) shows a jump of adoption in small firms from 25% in 2009 to an impressive 49% in 2012 (see Figure 2.3). It's clear that BIM has made meaningful inroads among small firms, and small architecture firms using a BIM workflow are still in the minority.

Nevertheless, as the case studies in this book and advanced practitioners all over the world can attest, BIM can have much to offer regardless of project scale. One of the obstacles to its greater adoption by the reluctant 70% or so of small firms that have yet to embrace BIM may be the perception that it is not suitable for design, an unfortunate misconception that this and previous work seeks to rectify. It's clear that even at the most pessimistic reported rate of under 30% adoption, over a quarter of small firms are using BIM for

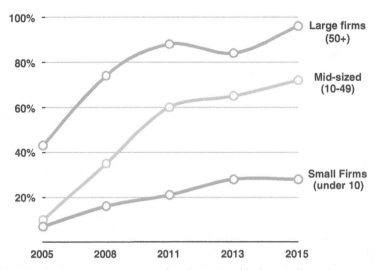

FIGURE 2.3 BIM adoption over recent years has increased in larger firms but appears to have plateaued in smaller ones.

Image courtesy of the American Institute of Architects, from the Firm Survey Report 2016, "The Business of Architecture."

their projects. That's a convincing number of small projects of all types being designed within a BIM workflow. What isn't known is *how* those firms use BIM. Do the majority use it only near the end of their processes, for late design development and construction documents alone, and employ other processes for schematic design and early design development? One suspects so. Nevertheless, there are now enough firms using a full-BIM workflow to make a convincing case that even while not all firms do use BIM, any firm *could*. This book makes the case that any firm probably *should*.

BIM-Authoring Platforms and Technologies

There are many BIM design software platforms currently available for AEC professionals, but there isn't necessarily a "one-size-fits-all" platform that works for all projects or all design team participants or even all locales. The purchase of a BIM platform should not be based merely on the tool's current capabilities and initial seat cost(s); rather, it should be viewed as an investment that will involve future evolutions, new content and file type generation, and continuous user training. While there are possibly dozens of software tools deemed BIM-capable for various stakeholders in the building industry, it seems appropriate to focus on the BIM tools currently being used by architects since they have the largest impact on building design and information workflows. The following BIM authoring tools are by no means exhaustive but do represent the majority of current adoption by the architecture profession in the United States. Each tool is described in terms of its current release, operating platform, user interface, product family, file organization, interoperability, extent of parametric component library, and scalability.

Autodesk's **Revit** is the most widely used BIM-authoring platform for building design in the United States. The software is typically updated on an annual cycle, usually released in early spring, and is only available for Windows operating systems. Like all BIM-authoring software, Revit is intended to allow the user a wide variety of modeling options to address the design and documentation needs of a diversity of building project typologies and workflows. Some complexity in the UX (user experience) is therefore inevitable, as for all BIM software, so the user should allocate resources (time and financial) to training. While improvements have been made to free-form modeling and conceptual design environments, Revit is best known for its capabilities in detailed design development and extracting coordinated technical documentation from the model (Figure 2.4). In addition to modeling and technical documentation, the software features a proprietary rendering engine, Raytracer, within the program for photorealistic view options. Autodesk prefers to license the software using a software-as-a-service (SaaS) model, where the user pays an annual subscription fee for access, and automatic annual upgrades, as well as access, are continually delivered as long as the user keeps paying the bill. Revit is offered as a single product at US$2,200 annually, but also as part of a larger collection of products related to architecture, engineering, and construction of buildings for about a 20%

FIGURE 2.4 Autodesk's Revit is best known for as BIM authoring software for large, complex projects. However, it's also suited to projects at other scales. Here, architect Julian Munoz's six-unit residential project in Colombia was designed, documented, and rendered entirely in Revit.

premium in the subscription cost (US$2,690) but noted significant discount over licensing each of the individual applications. Autodesk's BIM offerings in their AEC Collection includes:

- Revit (with Architecture, MEP, and Structural desktop tools, Structural Analysis cloud-based service, and Live for VR support)
- Navisworks Manage (for model analysis and 4D simulation)
- FormIt Pro (web and mobile app for schematic design)
- Insight (a plugin to Revit and FormIt for building energy modeling, simulation, and analysis)
- Recap Pro (point cloud management)
- Structural Bridge Design
- Advance Steel
- Robot Structural Analysis Professional
- Dynamo Studio (visual programming environment for all Autodesk tools)
- Autodesk Rendering (cloud-based rendering service)
- 3ds Max (general modeling, animation, and rendering)
- A360 Cloud Storage

To the user, it looks like a bargain as an initial investment, but the cost of ownership over time with the subscription program quickly adds up significantly. In addition, unless you are a professional with the personal ability to utilize the entire suite of software on a regular basis, the added software seems to be more useless bloatware than toolbox. Autodesk does reluctantly offer Revit as a standalone license, but it is not eligible for any discounted upgrades on an annual basis. This means if a user has purchased a 2017 version seat of Revit with this license, he/she must pay full price to get the 2018 or subsequent versions.

As with most BIM-authoring tools, Revit uses a single file database structure for storing and linking information. Thus project files become very large, very quickly, and performance can suffer as a result—especially when dealing with simultaneous multiuser collaboration. It is also an "object-based" system, utilizing common building concepts of walls, doors, slabs, etc., as the basic elements for assembling building designs. These concepts are referred to as "families" with user-definable geometries and parameters. Building product manufacturers utilize the family concept to supply an extensive online presence of model and brand-specific family libraries for use within Revit. The BIM database can be viewed in different modes whether as a model, a series of 2D views or drawings, and tabular (aka schedule) formats, maintaining relationships to each other so that a change in one "view" is automatically reflected in all other views of the same information. While the preference is to have third-party applications utilize the Revit API (application programming interface) to exchange geometry and information directly with the application, it does support importing/exporting various image, 2D, and 3D file types including Autodesk's own formats—DWG, DWF, FBX and ADSK—as well as open formats such as DXF, DGN, STL, SAT, SKP, BMP, JPG, JPEG, PNG, TIF, gbXML, and IFC.

Vectorworks Architect® by Vectorworks, Inc., a Nemetschek company, is another BIM authoring platform with a long history as a smaller but growing player in the US building industry, also well known in many international markets and primarily used by small- to medium-sized AEC firms working on projects of many different types and sizes. Vectorworks is updated on an annual basis, typically released in the fall with Service Pack updates throughout the following year and is available for Windows and Macintosh operating systems. The user interface offers a very flexible 2D/3D hybrid environment, which is beneficial for adapting to various design styles and workflows, but it does not enforce a single, strict, BIM workflow. Vectorworks is best known for its cross-platform support, numerous 3D modeling modes supported by the Siemen's Parasolid geometry kernel, and high-quality 2D output. Vectorworks supports robust free-form modeling with Boolean solids, NURBS curves and surfaces, and Sub-Division modeling. Photorealistic and artistic rendering is accomplished through the integrated Renderworks® functionality (see Figure 2.5), which is based on the MAXON Cinema4D® rendering engine, CineRender.

Vectorworks Architect is offered as a purchased perpetual license, where the user "owns" that version of the product in perpetuity. It is upgradable, at the user's choice, for a fee. As a valued-added option, users may choose to participate in the Service Select program, providing such benefits as regular delivery of updates and annual upgrades for a contracted fee, extended storage space for the Vectorworks Cloud Services (20GB instead of 5GB for the free version), premium technical support, and flexibility in renting seats on an as-needed basis, at monthly intervals. Vectorworks Architect is offered for US$3,000, while Designer is offered for slightly more. In addition, Vectorworks offers a mobile app, Nomad, for free, giving access to users' Cloud Services storage, as well as PDF viewing and markups and 3D visualization of designs, even in an immersive virtual reality mode, on mobile devices. Besides Architect, the Vectorworks platform has other industry-specific versions including Landmark® for landscape and site design, and Spotlight® for entertainment, set lighting, and exhibit design, all built on top of the Fundamentals platform. Vectorworks Designer® includes all industry tools, commands, and objects for those who need the widest array of tools to design anything and everything.

FIGURE 2.5 A Vectorworks Architect architectural project.
Image credit: SPLANN, lead architect Hamonic+Masson & Associés with A/LTA, associate architect.

Vectorworks also has a single file database structure for storing and linking information. As with Revit and ARCHICAD, performance suffers as projects and files grow large. Multiuser collaboration is similar to Revit, but with more administration over user permissions in accessing the different aspects of the project file. It is also an "object-based" system and has extensive data-rich object symbol libraries, allowing for a wide variety of building product manufacturer and user-created content. In addition, more complex object and process customization can be achieved through its Vectorscript programming language and Python scripting interface, which has been further extended with a visual programming component (similar to Grasshopper) known as Marionette. It does lack, however, certain building industry specific analytical tools for MEP and structure. Vectorworks Architect and Designer also include Energos, an energy analysis tool based on the PassivHaus methodology. The platform does have a C++ based API, but it is not necessary for most users to exchange information with other tools. Vectorworks supports the export and/or import of various image, 2D, and 3D file types including DOE-2, DXF, DWG, DWF, EPSF, HDRI, JPG, PNG, BMP, TIF, PDF, 3D PDF, Cinema 4D, COLLADA, FBX, IGES, KML, OBJ, Panorama, SAT, STEP, STL (for stereo lithography or 3D printing), Rhino 3DM, Parasolid X_T,

Web View, Vectorscript up to the five previous versions of Vectorworks, and comma- and tab-delimited worksheets, DIF, and SYLK. It is fully IFC compliant, a critical format for BIM interoperability among stakeholders.

ARCHICAD® by GRAPHISOFT, like Vectorworks a Nemetschek company, is the oldest dedicated BIM-authoring tool still available in many international markets, to date (see Figure 2.6). It tends to dominate in European countries, close to its corporate operations in Hungary. ARCHICAD is typically released annually in the summer and is available for both Windows and Macintosh operating systems.

The software can be purchased for approximately US$4,500 per seat license, upgraded for US$895, or rented on a monthly basis. GRAPHISOFT offers various extensions for ARCHICAD, including MEP Modeler, Virtual Building Explorer (for interactive 3D presentation), EcoDesigner (for energy analysis), and a plug-in for Artlantis (a third-party application for high-quality rendering). GRAPHISOFT has also developed a more economical and lightweight BIM software called ARCHICAD STAR(T) Edition (about US$2,000 per seat license), which is specifically designed for small architecture firms with limited features for modeling,

FIGURE 2.6 The University of Nottingham Ingenuity Centre designed by Bond Bryan Architects was modeled and documented in ARCHICAD.

visualization, collaboration, performance, and project organization. GRAPHISOFT lacks a dedicated structural BIM application, but like Vectorworks, relies on IFC for interoperability between various stakeholders and their tools. ARCHICAD supports various add-ons developed by third-party vendors to extend the functionality of the core BIM tool capabilities.

ARCHICAD's model information is managed by a centralized database, similar to Revit and Vectorworks. It supports importing/exporting file formats including DWG, DXF, DGN, DWF, and PDF. It also supports model data exporting to gbXML, DOE-2, RIUSKA, ARCHiPHISIK, OBDC, and IFC. The tool also supports direct links with SketchUp (3D modeler), Google Earth (virtual world visualization), and Cinema 4D (3D animation). ARCHICAD uses an "in-memory" system, which presents scalability issues for large projects, but models can be partitioned into smaller modules to make them manageable. In addition, GRAPHISOFT has developed the first BIM Server application, specifically intended to make large project collaboration easier and faster. ARCHICAD does have certain parametric modeling limitations in terms of automatic updating between objects. It also lacks modeling constraints and does not support association between modeling elements, which can be problematic for other analysis tools.

Bentley's **MicroStation** focuses on a wide range of solutions for AEC industries, including bridges, buildings, government, campuses, communications, utilities, factories, mining and metals, process manufacturing, power generation, rail and transit, roads, and water and wastewater (see Figure 2.7). The buildings category includes a family of products including Architecture, GenerativeComponents, Structural Modeler, Building Mechanical Systems, Building Electrical Systems, Facilities, and ProjectWise Navigator (for multiproject and multiuser collaboration). The current release of Bentley MicroStation is the CONNECT Edition (V10) and is only available on Windows operating systems. The software can be moderately expensive with single seat licenses priced at US$6,290 (includes MicroStation, passport for ProjectWise Navigator, Parametric Cell Studio, Space Planner, and Bentley Architecture). Existing MicroStation users can add Bentley Architecture for US$1,495. The user interface is large and nonintegrated, which makes it difficult to navigate and learn. Bentley Architecture features relatively fast conceptual design modeling and space planning capabilities. The software also features a powerful rendering engine for the production of high-quality images and animations within the application. Bentley Architecture supports importing/exporting formats including DGN, DWG, DXF, PDF, STEP, IGES, STL, and IFC. It also supports native Rhino and SketchUp modeling formats. The software has a relatively small parametric object library, which may be due to inconsistent object behaviors. Bentley Architecture features a distributed file structure to help manage large projects, but this type of file organization can be difficult to set up and manage.

FIGURE 2.7 An example of a Bentley MicroStation project, the Vadorrey Dock Multifunctional Building, Zaragoza, Spain. Design phase: Coro Garrido Fernández/Pedro Martin García (initial sketches/main project), Jose Antonio García Gómez (facilities), and Joaquín Lezcano (structure). Building phase: Pedro Martin García/Angel Muñoz Barrado (architects), Jose Ignacio Larraz, Fernando Bardavío (quantity surveyors).

Driving Model-Based Deliverables with the BIMForum Level of Development (LOD) Specification

Brian P. Skripac, Assoc. AIA, LEED AP BD+C, Vice President, CannonDesign

Although the development of building information models during the design, construct, and operate continuum has become a mainstay in the architecture, engineering, and construction industry, there is still a significant gap in how people actually define what a BIM is and how a BIM can be relied on and subsequently utilized by different project participants. In comparing the two images shown in Figure 2.8, people will certainly agree both are BIMs, but they both represent building systems, components, and assemblies at very different stages of development.

The BIMForum is an association of AEC industry stakeholders and the US chapter of buildingSMART International, and a core of its mission is to explore and deliver innovation and best practices through building information modeling. To address the challenge of defining the maturity of a BIM, the BIMForum has taken the lead, in collaboration with the Association of General Contractors of America (AGC) and the American Institute of Architects (AIA), in creating the Level of Development (LOD) Specification. Now in its fourth version, the LOD Specification 2016 is "a reference that enables practitioners in the AEC Industry to specify and articulate with a high degree of clarity the content and reliability of building information models at various stages in the

FIGURE 2.8 LOD lends flexibility to BIM and helps set modeling standards. Comparison of site and massing analysis including LOD 100 elements (left), and a more mature model of MEP systems with LOD 350 and 400 elements. Both are BIMs, and there's clearly a broad range of development possible.

Image credit CannonDesign.

design and construction process." This ability to have a common language and understanding of our deliverables is a key element in driving collaboration and setting expectations from each project's outset. Revisiting the images in Figure 2.8, we can see the massing model on the left is taking advantage of exterior wall, floor, and roof assemblies that do not exceed an LOD 100 while the MEP systems in the image on the right have evolved to include elements at LOD 350 and 400. This addresses a key aspect of the LOD specification, where it recognizes there is no such thing as an "LOD ### model" and a model does not achieve a certain LOD at a specific project milestone like SD, DD, or CD deliverables. Rather, LOD is all about the individual building systems, components and assemblies.

It's also important to realize the BIMForum LOD Specification is not a set of requirements. Instead, it's a language and a communication tool for model element authors to describe the "degree to which the element's geometry and attached information has been thought through," thus enabling other project participants to understand how much they can rely on that information.

Organized around the UniFormat Classification of Construction Systems and Assemblies, the BIMForum LOD Specification now includes references to the associated MasterFormat and OmniClass section to bring a more holistic approach to defining a model's development. Within this organizational structure, the LOD Specification breaks down each construction system and assembly by verbally and graphically outlining how that element evolves across each level of development (see Figure 2.9). Each section outlines its unique geometric aspects, but for consistency all components refer back to the fundamental LOD definitions listed below:

LOD 100. The Model Element may be graphically represented in the Model with a symbol or other **generic representation**, but does not satisfy the requirements for LOD 200. Information related to the Model Element (i.e., cost per square foot, tonnage of HVAC, etc.) can be derived from other Model Elements. BIMForum interpretation: *LOD 100 elements are not geometric representations. Examples are information attached to other model elements or symbols showing the existence of a component but not its shape, size, or precise location. Any information derived from LOD 100 elements must be considered approximate.*

LOD 200. The Model Element is graphically represented within the Model as a **generic system**, object, or assembly with **approximate** quantities, size, shape, location, and orientation. Nongraphic information may also be attached to the Model Element. BIMForum interpretation: *At this LOD elements are generic placeholders. They may be recognizable as the components they represent, or they may be volumes for space reservation. Any information derived from LOD 200 elements must be considered approximate.*

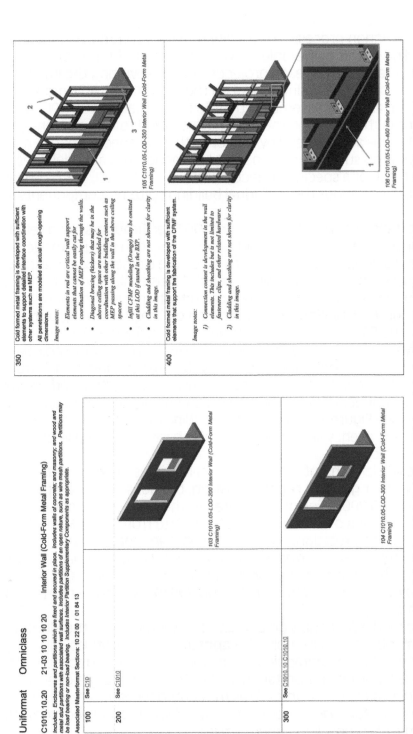

FIGURE 2.9 An example of defining LOD, in this case for an interior fixed partition (cold-form metal framing), one of many from the BIMForum LOD Specification. The LOD Specification clarifies definitions and seeks to eliminate ambiguity in interpreting the development and reliability of elements in a BIM.

Image credit BIMForum.

LOD 300. The Model Element is graphically represented within the Model as a **specific system**, object, or assembly in terms of quantity, size, shape, location, and orientation. Nongraphic information may also be attached to the Model Element. BIMForum interpretation: *The quantity, size, shape, location, and orientation of the element as designed can be measured directly from the model without referring to nonmodeled information such as notes or dimension call-outs. The project origin is defined and the element is located accurately with respect to the project origin.*

LOD 350. The Model Element is graphically represented within the Model as a **specific system**, object, or assembly in terms of quantity, size, shape, orientation, and **interfaces with other building systems.** Nongraphic information may also be attached to the Model Element. BIMForum interpretation: *Parts necessary for coordination of the element with nearby or attached elements are modeled. These parts will include such items as supports and connections. The quantity, size, shape, location, and orientation of the element as designed can be measured directly from the model without referring to nonmodeled information such as notes or dimension call-outs.*

LOD 400. The Model Element is graphically represented within the Model as a **specific system**, object, or assembly in terms of size, shape, location, quantity, and orientation **with detailing, fabrication, assembly, and installation information.** Nongraphic information may also be attached to the Model Element. BIMForum interpretation: *An LOD 400 element is modeled at sufficient detail and accuracy for fabrication of the represented component. The quantity, size, shape, location, and orientation of the element as designed can be measured directly from the model without referring to nonmodeled information such as notes or dimension call-outs.*

LOD 500. The Model Element is a **field verified representation** in terms of size, shape, location, quantity, and orientation. Nongraphic information may also be attached to the Model Elements. BIMForum interpretation: *Since LOD 500 relates to field verification and is not an indication of progression to a higher level of model element geometry or nongraphic information, this Specification does not define or illustrate it.*

The LOD Specification is not merely about geometry; it also takes into consideration the necessary nongraphical or associate attribute information. This section outlines both baseline and additional attributes that merge with the overall geometric LOD definition. While it is not possible to outline every piece of nongraphical information that could ever be needed, the BIMForum has defined the baseline elements for each LOD and then lists other additional attributes for use by the project team.

While this information is in place for project teams to take advantage of, we must also consider how these important strategies and definitions become part of our contractual obligations for all project participants and clients to understand what we are working to deliver. With this in mind, the AIA Contract Documents committee has developed the following documents:

- **E203-2013**, Building Information Modeling and Digital Data Exhibit
- **G201-2013**, Project Digital Data Protocol Form
- **G202-2013**, Project Building Information Modeling Protocol Form

While the E203 is the actual exhibit to the contract, it enables the use of the G202, which gives the project team the opportunity to indicate the LOD to which each building systems, components, and assemblies (model elements) in the model shall be developed at each identified project milestone. This document also enables teams to outline which model element author will be responsible for managing and coordinating the development of those specific model elements throughout the course of the project.

It's easy to see that as our industry has continued to evolve the idea of building information modeling (a verb), the topics has rapidly moved past a conversation of a technology being used to deliver a set of construction documents. Now we are more holistically focused on how a building information model (a noun) is a deliverable that has process and contractual implications that need to be defined. Fortunately, the BIMForum and AIA are working to create specification and contract language for the AEC industry to explore and define these opportunities that can advance the building industry.

These larger ideas play in important role in the ongoing design process, enabling the architect to convey design intent in a consistent way, referencing a language (LOD) that has been adopted by the industry. These definitions are able to remove the ambiguity and interpretation in the design process so misunderstandings can be avoided. For instance, the question "Is that the exact chair that we'll have in the meeting room?" might come up in a presentation. The answer would be "No, that chair is a placeholder—it's a generic representation at LOD 200. Our team will model that specific element at LOD 300 for the next project deliverable milestone where you'll see the exact version of the chair." While a simple example, it's clear how this impacts the client's understanding, the rest of the design team, and others who may be bidding or providing other feedback on the project.

Industry Foundation Classes

Digital interoperability is nothing new. The Internet itself would not exist without standardized protocols and schemas like HTTP and HTML to encode, transfer, store, decode, and display all the data we have and continue to share around the world. Thanks to such interoperable standards, the data of the Internet is bigger and more important than the tools used to create, present, and consume the information, no matter the form of the data, the device, or the interface. Logically, the AEC industry's data ought to work in much the same way. Industry Foundation Classes (IFC) provides that opportunity as a standard description of the built environment that can understood by people and machines, no matter the geography, market, or sector of the AEC industry. IFC is the product of buildingSMART International, a global initiative to standardize and proselytize the digitization of the building industry and the ability to leverage the information of a project throughout its entire lifecyle. For IFC to be effective, there must be a willingness to see its value and embrace it. Note that this is not an exhaustive treatise on IFC, a topic that could itself be the subject of an entire book (or more).

IFC: Basic Concepts

Rather than being a proprietary software technology or single application, BIM is clearly a digital and social process. Individual firms are free to select whatever BIM authoring (or analysis or coordination) application(s) that suit them. To allow a rich ecosystem of BIM applications to thrive and avoid technological strangleholds, IFC has evolved as a mechanism for interoperability. *IFC is a nonproprietary, open standard means of describing the built environment and freely exchanging and/or storing that information digitally: geometry plus information.*

BIM objects need to be describable, particularly when out of context and/or unfamiliar to the viewer. IFC allows the capturing of many of a building object's characteristics, from its 3D geometry to the important information attached to that geometry, defining what it is. IFC is a means of describing all physical and nonphysical aspects of the design, procurement, assembly, and operation of a building over its entire life cycle. More than just a file format, it is a "language," like Esperanto, with semantics and rules of grammar. More simply put, IFC is like an HTML (hypertext markup language) standard, but for the built environment. Critically, IFC is:

- **Open**, available to any software developer and publicly documented.

- **Neutral**, neither favoring nor biasing any single application, suite of applications, software vendor or developer, hardware platform or operating system. IFC is also multilingual.

- **Nonproprietary**, and importantly not a native file format for any application, thus ensuring its continued openness and neutrality.

The processes and technologies possible to "do BIM" are pointing to an over-arching concept that ties them all together, that of **interoperability**—the ability to exchange and make use of building data among multiple stakeholders. To achieve this, the geometry descriptions in IFC include two main categories of 3D geometry representations, each comprising specific subsets: solid geometry (also known as CSG) and Surface/BREP (Boundary REPresentation), as shown in Figure 2.10.

As an open standard for capturing and exchange industry data, IFC allows the leveraging of all the technology available to designers and consumers today. These products cover the entire spectrum of the construction industry from architectural, structural, and building services design, to energy analysis, cost analysis, construction management, facility/asset management, and data servers. (As part of its mission, buildingSMART International seeks to address the entire life cycle of a building project, expressed as the quatrefoil in its logo, from inception through construction and operations.)

BIM applications are not just content creation applications but include ways to view, report, analyze, and document BIM in ways that are important to a particular participant in the BIM process with a given data set or model. A large number of BIM products support IFC, but only a small fraction are certified by buildingSMART International as IFC compliant. The certification gives software users confidence that an IFC-based data exchange with the software in question has been tested by an industry authority and is functional and technically capable of correctly exporting and/or importing IFC files. However, certification does not guarantee that an IFC file generated from an application will unfailingly be viable or correct, due to the potential for user mismodeling or inappropriately applying data to the model. There is still room for error, as users may incorrectly encode information in the BIM tool and thwart the tools' certified capabilities. As a result, even with software that is certified to be technically able to correctly produce and interpret IFC files, validation is often required. Validation soft-ware like Solibri Model Checker and Navisworks Manage still have an important role to play in validating IFC models, helping ensure that the correct scope and format of information is being exchanged. Such validation software also includes features to view, coordinate, and analyze federated BIM models, even gener-ating clash detection and quantity take-off reports. In the end, certification is a significant step forward, though, enabling users around the world to effec-tively share BIM data regardless of the BIM authoring platforms they use, or even languages they speak.

The commitment to IFC by the vendor community has been strengthened through participation in the IFC 2×3 certification. It includes all the major BIM authoring application vendors including products from such international players as Autodesk, Bentley, and Nemetschek, and as of this writing spanning 22 ven-dors and 33 applications, supporting architectural, structural, MEP (aka building

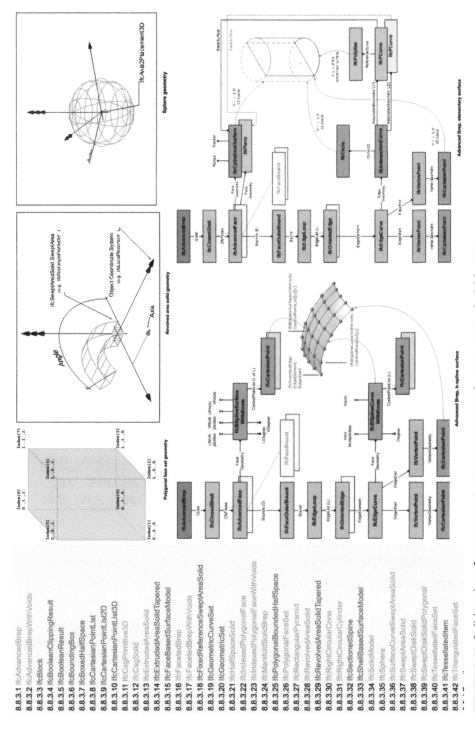

FIGURE 2.10 Solid and surface geometry types commonly represented within IFC.

Image credit: Jeffrey Ouellette; IFC modeling representations by Thomas Liebich for buildingSMART.

services), model viewing, and facilities management workflows. In addition, IFC4 (the newest version of IFC) is also being certified and participation from the same previous group of vendors has already begun.

One can think of IFC-compliant BIM processes as the natural evolution of building information modeling. A digital model of project that lacks data (the "I" in BIM), may be visually captivating, but without that data the analytic opportunities are minimal as best (for the value of data analysis in BIM processes, see the case studies in Chapters 5 and 6 especially, as well as *BIM in Small-Scale Sustainable Design*). A data-rich digital model is at the heart of BIM. Interoperable BIM, enabled by IFC, broadens the reach and thus value of the model, extending it to colleagues, collaborators, and clients.

Technical Details

As a data schema that catalogues all the configuration, semantics, domains, processes, relationships, and attributes/properties that fully describe the multitude of details of the elements of a building, IFC must fundamentally address building geometry, both 3D and 2D.

IFC does so with **STEP** (Standard for the Exchange of Product Model data, formally known as ISO 10303; IFC itself is ISO 16739). STEP includes definitions for an object's or assembly's *bounding box* and body, the latter describable as a BREP (boundary consisting of surfaces), a Clipped Solid (the product of a Boolean operation like additive or subtractive modeling), a Swept Solid (a profile revolved along an arc path), and/or a Linear Extrude solid. In addition, STEP can accommodate a vector footprint, faceting, survey points, and mapped item representation.

But BIM objects need more to be useful beyond simply describing their geometry for visualization. Information, data with context and meaning, needs to be tied to the geometry to make it truly useful (Figure 2.11). This information includes:

- **Semantics**, including *entities* (object definitions) and *types* (common definitions for multiple instances).

- **Attributes**, such as identity, properties (Property Sets or PSets), and classification.

- **Relationships**, including *hierarchies* (spatial or organizational), physical connections (e.g., wall-to-wall, wall-to-slab, column-to-beam, etc.), and group connections, be they systems (HVAC, water supply, water sewer, etc.) or zones (e.g., security, use, thermal control, etc.).

- **Ownership** (e.g., owner, designer, supplier, manufacturer, contractor, etc.).

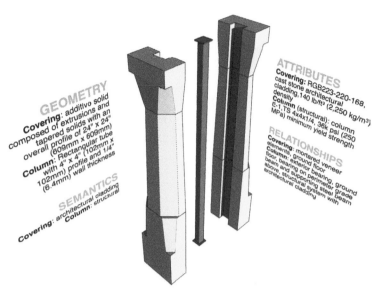

GEOMETRY
Covering: additivo solid composed of extrusions and tapered solids with an overall profile of 24" x 24" (609mm x 609mm)
Column: Rectangular tube with 4" X 4" (102mm x 102mm) profile and 1/4" (6.4mm) wall thickness

SEMANTICS
Covering: architectural cladding
Column: structural

ATTRIBUTES
Covering: RGB223-220-168, cast stone architectural cladding,140 lb/ft³ (2,250 kg/m³) density
Column (structural): column E-1,TS 4x4x1/4, 36k psi (250 MPa) minimum yield strength

RELATIONSHIPS
Covering: mortared veneer elements, ground floor
Column: exterior bearing, ground floor, bearing on perimeter grade beam and supporting steel grade above, structural system with architectural cladding

FIGURE 2.11 The contextualization of IFC data is critical to representing buildings and their components beyond merely obvious geometry.

The IFC specification was created for the built environment and has data structures such as those outlined in Figure 2.12 that reflect this context. IFC can thus fully describe the geometry with information that can be used for determining cost, aesthetics, sequencing, and structural integrity, among other useful analyses necessary throughout the life cycle of the building object, component, or assembly. An IFC file of a building indicates how the parts of a building relate to the overall project, how the building relates to its site, with limits and parameters meant to distinguish it from other buildings potentially on the same site. The full specification of IFC is a repository of schema definitions for all disciplines and life cycle, A "Model View Definition" is a subset, one that satisfies one or many purposes.

While the IFC standard specifies how to organize built environment data according to rational definitions, there are multiple ways to code that data in machine-readable form. IFC-STP (.ifc) is the *express* version, enabling the use of complex geometry and data structures, based on the manufactured product interoperability standard STEP. IFC is actually a building industry adaptation of that specification. **ifcXML** is an XML-based version of the same data, but in a format more directly and widely supported by the larger computing industry and is thus more accessible to web-based apps and devices than the STEP version. And **ifcZIP** is a version that is able to wrap either an .ifc or .ifcxml file

FIGURE 2.12 There are multiple representations of a BIM according to its use for reference, design, construction, structural analysis, energy analysis, and facilities management.

together with linked images and/or documents into a single file archive. And these three file formats are not the end; as the AEC industry attracts the interest of more computer scientists, new proposals are arising to align AEC industry data practices with those typically found in the rest of the broader global computing industry.

It may be clear that the IFC standard is not static even while it is in active use. Like most actively used digital standards, it is a work in progress, evolving as more industry needs are identified and general computing technology matures. It has been an ongoing effort for over 20 years and counting, with 12 companies initially forming an alliance to improve the state of interoperability between third-party products developed for the Autodesk AutoCADD platform, eventually blossoming into an effort of true multiplatform interoperability on a global scale (see Figures 2.13 and 2.14).

The past several years have been focused on IFC version 4. The current official ISO standard as of this writing, IFC4, has little support among current BIM

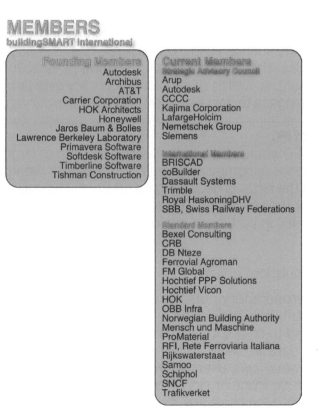

MEMBERS
buildingSMART International

Founding Members
Autodesk
Archibus
AT&T
Carrier Corporation
HOK Architects
Honeywell
Jaros Baum & Bolles
Lawrence Berkeley Laboratory
Primavera Software
Softdesk Software
Timberline Software
Tishman Construction

Current Members
Strategic Advisory Council
Arup
Autodesk
CCCC
Kajima Corporation
LafargeHolcim
Nemetschek Group
Siemens

International Members
BRISCAD
coBuilder
Dassault Systems
Trimble
Royal HaskoningDHV
SBB, Swiss Railway Federations

Standard Members
Bexel Consulting
CRB
DB Nteze
Ferrovial Agroman
FM Global
Hochtief PPP Solutions
Hochtief Vicon
HOK
OBB Infra
Norwegian Building Authority
Mensch und Maschine
ProMaterial
RFI, Rete Ferroviaria Italiana
Rijkswaterstaat
Samoo
Schiphol
SNCF
Trafikverket

FIGURE 2.13 The founders of the IFC data standard and IFC participants today.

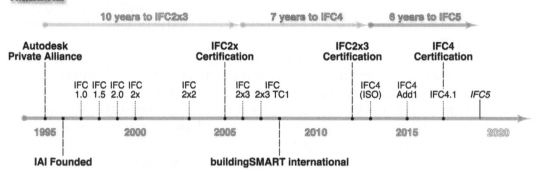

FIGURE 2.14 A timeline of IFC adoption.

software products. That will change, however, as more software implementations are certified. Moreover, version 4 offers many changes and improvements to how data is captured, made relevant, and exchanged. One of the most significant changes is the current effort to add more of the built environment—infrastructure such as roads, tunnels, railways, and bridges. Initially, this is manifesting itself in the new data sets for alignment, enabling the correct geospatial placement, as well as dimensional accuracy over large distances, while accounting for change in terrain elevation and even the curvature of the earth.

Design Benefits of IFC

On the face of it, IFC would seem to be only of concern to large firms or those with design processes encompassing multiple disciplines working closely together (though the latter is becoming increasingly common even for small firms). Yet even for the smaller firm or design studio, there are two important areas impacted by IFC in particular and interoperability in general:

1. Open BIM
2. Analysis and simulation

Open BIM. Interoperability puts the emphasis and primary value on BIM data (the geometry, attributes, and relationships of BIM objects) and the processes and workflows used to create it. The particular software tools used to create and consume the data are secondary though important. By emphasizing the value of data and workflows, users are free to select appropriate software tools for their particular discipline or workflow, creating and transferring resulting content for another discipline's use, or consuming data from another source and transforming it while maintaining its connection and context to the original purpose. Open and ubiquitous data access does not limit the quality or extents of BIM data.

IFC-based interoperability also has a significant impact on software developers. Vendors are often challenged with data exchange between disparate systems. For example, the resources required for all architectural BIM authoring software to support connections with all structural analysis and modeling packages from markets around the world would likely be prohibitive. By focusing on the importance of the data, there's a significant impact on the development process for existing and new software developers. Moving away from multiple, single-use, proprietary APIs to a single open data formatting and exchange standard can lower the threshold for developers and their customers to connect to the greater BIM ecosystem.

The choice of IFC and open BIM is much like we use the Internet, where the tools and devices we use to create, transfer, and consume information are highly varied and secondary to the data itself. Moreover, IFC and open BIM remove restrictions for participation in a BIM project. By specifying the use of IFC for BIM data exchange, any member of the project team is free to use whatever tools they prefer, provided that they are IFC compatible.

(**Note:** there are three homonyms often associated with interoperability and BIM. **OPEN BIM™** (all uppercase) is a marketing program established by GRAPHISOFT and shared by other software vendors; **openBIM®** (a single word, with "open" all lowercase) is an official buildingSMART International registered trademark and specifically refers to IFC; and **open BIM**, a generic term consisting of two words normally capitalized. As this book is intended for a broad audience of architects and designers with no particular software platforms in mind, the generic term is used and intended—"Open BIM" at the beginning of sentence, "open BIM" otherwise.)

On the other hand, "closed" BIM puts the primary emphasis on the tool, or platform, in which data is created and consumed. Such data can only be accessed when the same platform, or its variants, are used. The extents and quality of the data depend entirely on the technical capabilities of the selected platform. Any software tool that is limited in its compatibility with the selected BIM platform is omitted, even if it may be important to a member of the team or to a particular design workflow. Closed BIM also compromises the ability to share information between platforms.

When used as intended, IFC works today for model referencing, validation, and coordination, allowing users to exchange and share BIM models without disrupting their preferred software, and managing changes with BCF (BIM collaboration format, using bcfXML files and a RESTful web service using bcfAPI).

There are a number of key benefits to developing, supporting, and using open standard technologies:

□ **Intellectual property ownership and security.** The designer's work and expertise, and thereby value, is encapsulated in the BIM, a comprehensive digital database of every aspect of the building, from the overall parti down to the smallest detail. How is that data accessed after it has been created? Does the architect have to rely on a software vendor to maintain access to that valuable database, now and in the future? Shouldn't the content authors own and control the content, not an application developer? IFC does not rely on the integrity of a single application file format controlled by a particular vendor, nor is the data hostage to future support or compatibility with a subsequent version of the BIM software. IFC data is also not reliant on the stability of a particular application or product, nor specialized application extensions, plug-ins, or utilities and their potential versioning.

□ **Portability.** Think of BIM and IFC like the Internet and HTML. Information on the Internet is readily accessible with little effort because all the software tools support the reading and writing of a standard machine language, HTML, for the display of the information. As the technology becomes more capable, flexible, and powerful, these standards evolve, in turn giving more users improved access and experiences from more devices and applications. IFC makes building data portable, flexible enough to access from many different platforms—even including the web, via IFCXML.

□ **Integrity.** Numerous tools can read and display IFC files. Some are able to automatically check the quality and comprehensiveness of an IFC file, based on user-defined criteria or rules. Moreover, all the information the design team has created can be safeguarded, by using IFC not just as an active information exchange format but also for data archiving.

□ **Extensibility.** Finally, IFC is an extensible option. More data can be added to the BIM over time and as needed, by any stakeholder and IFC-compliant tool, as the scope of BIM or the project expands. The IFC-based BIM of a project today is merely the beginning of a database for more information to be added, queried and extracted, edited, and recompiled in the future.

There are, of course, limitations to IFC. Perhaps most obviously, IFC is strictly for BIM, not 2D documentation workflows. Any IFC entity is composed of geometry plus IFC data; IFC elements are not parametric or native to any BIM authoring platform. Users shouldn't expect an IFC-imported column, for example, to be easily parametrically editable as a native column object would be in the BIM authoring software. There's actually some value in that. A structural engineer sharing a structural model with an architect likely would not want the architect to edit that model. The architect needs it for coordination and to provoke a design dialogue, but it's really the engineer's responsibility to create and edit that structural model. Having the architect reference IFC structural elements helps maintain respective authorship among design disciplines. As a result, in its current implementation, IFC is not intended for design "round-tripping." That is, members of the design team on different BIM platforms should not expect to be able to collaborate so closely on the federated BIM model that they can readily edit each other's work (see Figure 2.15).

Analysis and Simulation. The needs and preferences of users within the entire AECO (AEC + occupancy) spectrum are extraordinarily diverse, and that diversity is still growing as BIM adoption expands and more professionals grasp how they can leverage BIM's data and technology. If we accept the idea that BIM is broad, comprising the formulation, design, analysis, encoding, decoding, fabrication, simulation, and management of a project, then we must also recognize that open standards support such a varied set of workflows. For the design-oriented practice, even one working fairly independently of "big BIM" processes, open BIM increases design opportunities. IFC gives designers access to a greater array of simulation and analysis tools, enabling improved performance-based design (Figure 2.16).

Quantitative validation of qualitative design processes is discussed at length in *BIM in Small-Scale Sustainable Design*. That previous book makes the case for performance-based analysis—in this instance energy efficiency and sustainable resources—as a source of architectural formalism. While many advocates of performance-oriented computational design insist that they are not engaged in formalism, it doesn't have to be an either/or proposition. Architecture can both pursue formal sensibilities and arise out of performance-based design processes. Some of the design opportunities available out of an IFC BIM workflow include:

- **Thermal performance simulation.** As BIM has evolved, more architectural BIM authoring software applications have integrated thermal performance analysis directly in the application. This is distinct from thermal *modeling*, which tends to require hour-by-hour simulation of building envelope performance based on climate data. Built-in thermal analysis tools like Revit's Insight, Vectorworks' Energos, and ARCHICAD's EcoDesigner allow early design performance feedback, but they are not true energy modelers. Open BIM allows exporting of the model to IES VE, OpenStudio, and Simergy, to name a few. The number and quality of BEM (building energy modeling) applications able to read IFC have been increasing.

FIGURE 2.15 An IFC model compared (above) to its BIM-authoring source (below). The IFC model is not intended to be an editable or even presentable building information model. Rather, its value lies in the exchange of project-critical information, from geometry to typological classification of model elements.

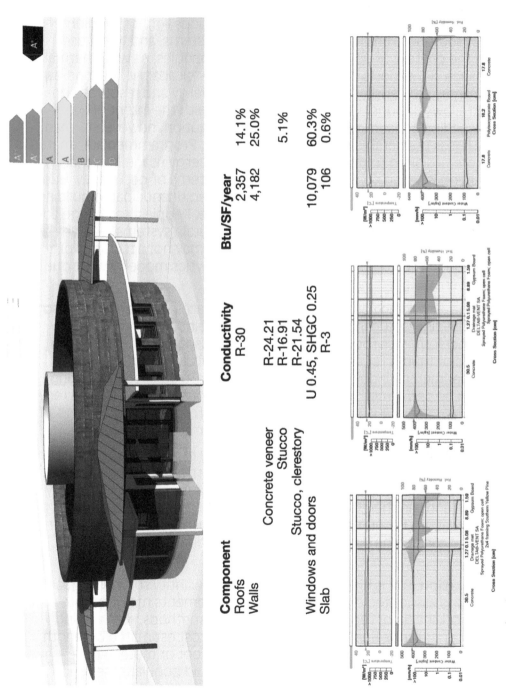

Component		Conductivity		Btu/SF/year	
Roofs		R-30		2,357	14.1%
Walls				4,182	25.0%
	Concrete veneer	R-24.21			
	Stucco	R-16.91		5.1%	
	Stucco, clerestory	R-21.54			
Windows and doors		U 0.45, SHGC 0.25		10,079	60.3%
Slab		R-3		106	0.6%

FIGURE 2.16 Simulation and performance analysis options are available through IFC and open BIM that would otherwise be inaccessible within the native BIM-authoring application. Here, Vectorworks Energos analysis was performed on a Revit model via IFC export/import, while a proposed wall assembly was analyzed with WUFI, a one-dimensional hygrothermic modeler for heat and moisture migration over time. Capital Area Rural Transportation System (CARTS) Eastside Bus Plaza project design by McCann Adams Studio and Jackson McElhaney Architects; energy and sustainability analysis by the author.

◻ **Energy and resource consumption analysis.** Hand in hand with thermal performance, overall energy analysis includes lighting, equipment power consumption, onsite energy generation systems, and water use, all within the context of usage and occupancy schedules. As with thermal performance, IFC exports of BIM expands the user's capability beyond early design analysis. Obviously, simulation of overall energy and resource consumption allows designers to modify the design with the intent of meeting or exceeding consumption goals. A word of caution, however: human behavior is less predictable than building systems. Programmed automated controls are designed to optimize comfort and energy usage, but that programming is based on assumptions about patterns of occupancy. Human behavior may not be so easily predictable, however; unanticipated building use schedules can have an effect on performance. People also change control settings in unexpected ways, or may not maintain systems regularly or properly, and so on. As a result, energy modeling may not accurately predict real-world performance—not out of poor physics modeling, but due to occupant behavior.

◻ **Daylighting.** Providing natural light for interior spaces saves energy; it also enhances building occupants' experience to the point of demonstrably improved performance for commercial and office spaces. While there are simple rules of thumb for estimating useful natural daylight penetration based on perimeter window sizes and locations, more detailed daylighting analysis can be performed within BIM authoring software using built-in rendering engines. More quantitative work is possible from a BIM model imported to daylight analysis software like IES Virtual Environment or OpenStudio.

◻ **Zoning, human occupancy, and movement.** 3D models (whether BIM or not) are very useful for verifying compliance for form-based zoning ordinances. BIM space objects required for GSA compliance contain occupancy information and can therefore be used within BIM for occupancy analysis, and egress calculations for number and size of openings, for example. Software like SimTread can also be used for emergency and disaster evacuation simulation.

◻ **Cost simulation.** BIM is highly suited to QS/QTO (quantity surveying/quantity take-offs) and associated cost analysis. Building elements may populate cost estimate worksheets or reports using a variety of methods, with varying degrees of granularity. For example, walls can be cost estimated by length (ignoring height) using an average cost per linear foot or meter. Alternately, the total surface area of the overall wall could populate the report, for greater precision. Finally, each wall component's area (structural core, sheathing, insulation, interior and exterior finishes) could be calculated and ascribed a material and labor value for a very detailed cost analysis. (Note that there is a difference between precise and accurate; an estimate could be very granular and *precise*, and still be less *accurate* than a coarser but more realistic estimate.) In addition to cost estimating, procurement and life cycle data may be associated with BIM objects, and architectural and MEP schedules may be exported to comply with the COBie format for owner's asset management.

- **Coordination/clash detection.** One of BIM's most recognized features is the ability to combine multiple models, each generated by a design discipline (architecture, structural engineering, civil engineering, MEP engineering) and compare them for clashes or collision. Commonly, clash detection is performed in a dedicated model checker, dedicated BIM software like Solibri or Navisworks, that is able to import, view, compare, and generate clash detection reports. Model checkers also verify the data integrity of the federated model, helping team members ensure that their respective models are properly classified and constructed:

  - **Model checkers** are full-featured software applications. While not BIM authoring software, they perform important "big BIM" functions: viewing, validation, deficiency detection, data mining, custom rulesets for code checking, reporting, and BCF support.

  - **Model viewers** are generally free versions of model checkers, and allow just that: viewing the (typically IFC) model without access to the authoring software's license. Low-cost model viewers also allow viewing of BCF, BIM Collaboration Format files.

      Model checkers are an integral part of BIM quality assurance/quality control (QA/QC), and are critical to managing data sharing.

Other BIM Interoperability

There are entire books to be written on BIM and interoperability, and two important topics bear some discussion here: COBie and the use of planning guides.

COBie

The Construction Operations Building Information Exchange is a data standard created by the US Army Corps of Engineers as part of the larger US National BIM Standards (NBIMS-US). COBie is an information exchange aimed at a building's managed assets. It captures important data, typically for large facilities, that is important to the owner's operation of the facility for its life cycle, through the design, procurement, and construction phases of a project. Being the first formal buildingSMART IE (information exchange) adopted in the NBIMS-US, it has already made an impact in the way BIM is used to deliver many public-sector projects as well as large private-sector facilities like hospitals and higher education buildings, and has been adopted in the United States, the United Kingdom, and Singapore. The US General Services Administration has provided the specifications for data exchange developed with their experience as the US government's landlord to hundreds of millions of square feet of facilities around the country and world. There's now a Life Cycle Information Exchange for Product Data (LCie) that defines a COBieLite XML subschema for products and product type data exchanges throughout the facility life cycle to be used for developing next generation of mobile and desktop applications for management of COBie data.

COBie data is about the information ascribed to managed building assets like lighting, plumbing, various selection, and mechanical components. From a designer's perspective, COBie data is associated with schedules: lighting, plumbing, equipment, room finishes, and so forth. COBie-compliant BIM-authoring software automatically assigns unique identifiers for all assets for scheduling purposes, or the user can assign them. The advantage to a building owner is that all assets are documented according to a predictable format, and hand-off manuals can be delivered electronically in a searchable database. Even if a designer does not anticipate needing COBie compliance for a current project, it's a good practice to implement BIM scheduling of assets, for greater accuracy now and to facilitate a future transition to IFC/COBie-compliant work.

Planning Guides

The *BIM Project Execution Planning Guides for Project Delivery Teams and Facility Owners* provide a structured approach for project delivery teams to implement BIM workflows and technologies, as well as guiding facility owners to plan adoption of BIM in their organizations to manage future projects (see Figure 2.17). The guides, and affiliated content, provide owners and the project team the tools to:

◻ Define what BIM means to the project and team and setting goals for the use of BIM.

◻ Lay out the processes used at each phase of the project. This allows the team to anticipate and plan for the particulars of BIM data exchange, provides a mechanism for decision making on such data, and allows for the coordination of schedules and even contingency plans for data exchange problems.

◻ Define the scope of BIM data to be shared and prescribe the extents and format of that data at any given point of the design process, including what components are to be modeled, what is to be excluded, what a particular set of data can be used for, or even what uses for certain data sets are prohibited.

SECTION G: QUALITY CONTROL

Quality Control Checks:

The following checks should be performed to meet quality expectations.

CHECKS	DEFINITION	FREQUENCY
VISUAL CHECK	Confirm that there are no unintended model components and the design intent has been followed.	Ongoing
INTERFERENCE CHECK	Detect problems in the model where two building components are clashing.	Ongoing
STANDARDS CHECK	Confirm that the BIM and AEC CADD Standard have been followed (fonts, dimensions, line styles, levels/layers, etc.).	Weekly
MODEL INTEGRITY CHECKS	Validate and confirm that the Project Facility Data set has no undefined, incorrectly defined or duplicated elements, control the quantity of major errors, and monitor file size to maintain project efficiency.	Weekly
MODEL HEALTH ASSESSMENTS (MHA)	Building on Model Integrity checks, utilize MHAs assess model viability and digital coherence. This will include: view counts, group counts, error and warning clearing, and provide a report denoting non compliant elements and corrective action plans.	Per deliverable

Model Accuracy and Tolerances:

Models should include all appropriate dimensioning as needed for design intent, analysis, and construction. The following modeling standards are to be met:

- All objects are to be modeled to a tolerance of 1/256".
- Angles shall be modeled to a tolerance of .001°.
- Dimension tolerance shall be 1/8" and .01°.

FIGURE 2.17 A sample from the *BIM Execution Planning Guides*. Respective roles and expectations for deliverables are clearly defined for smoother project delivery. Image courtesy of Justin Dowhower.

▫ Finally, these planning guides even provide for a "meta" cataloging of the design infrastructure—the people, technologies, and design team assets available—and help the team determine what resources are needed in order to fulfill the design team's goals for the use of BIM for the project. This would include project management decisions including the acquisition of technologies, training of personnel, communication protocols, and so forth.

SECTION H: MODEL STRUCTURE

1. File Naming Structure:

FILE NAMES FOR MODELS SHOULD BE FORMATTED AS:	
PROJECT NUMBER - DISCIPLINE.rvt (example: Proj. Name-#########-DISCIPLINE.rvt)	
ARCHITECTURAL MODEL	AACU_170800000_ARCH.rvt
STRUCTURAL MODEL	AACU_170800000_STRUCT.rvt
MEP MODEL	AACU_170800000_MEP.rvt
IT / SECURITY	AACU_170800000_IT.rvt
CIVIL	AACU_170800000_CIV.dwg
LANDSCAPE	AACU_170800000_LAND.dwg

2. Measurement and Coordinate Systems:

The measurement system shall be imperial. The finish floor elevation of level one shall be modeled at 100'-0" in the Z axis. Consultant files shall use the X and Y axes from the Architectural model, and will be imported using Origin-to-Origin.

3. Sheet Numbering:

Sheets shall be numbered as follows: Discipline indicator followed by a two-digit number that represents the drawing type followed by a dash followed by a two-digit sheet number and where applicable followed by a single letter designation of the plan segment area. EX: A02-01A, P02-01A, FS02-01A, etc.

Discipline indicators shall be as follows:
Civil	C
Landscape	L
Structural	S
Architectural/Interiors	A
Mechanical	M
Electrical	E
Plumbing	P
Audio/Visual	AV

FIGURE 2.17 (*Continued*)

Chapter 3

What Tools Mean

In a discussion of (digital) design processes, one phrase is sure to raise my hackles: "It's just a tool." The expression is both dismissive and thoughtless. The deprecatory "just" relegates discussions of tool using to a matter of mere preferences, trivial like your favorite brand of soft drink. And the expression is thoughtless because it refuses to consider that the relationship of user to tool may be in a sense dialectic. As an analogy, Marx wrote that he took Hegel and "stood him on his head." By that he meant, among other things, that individuals and particulars give rise to generalizations, rather than ideals governing human behavior. For Marx, history was the accrual of a myriad of human actions, rather than human activity being given by invisible forces. In both the Marxist and Hegelian view, however, causality is a single vector—the arrow just points in opposite directions. What if human activity were more like a synthesis of these views: humans both collectively create a culture as function of their individual activities, and human culture informs the boundaries of what individual actions are possible, or at least condoned?

Back to the use of tools—in our case, design tools—consider that there may be a similar dialectic at work. Obviously the hand manipulates the tool. And clearly the design of the tool—intentional or otherwise—predisposes certain operations over others. And could not the use of a particular tool in turn prejudice the user?

Introduction

A tool is an implement or device intended for a specific function, often inferred to be handheld and thereby a haptic extension of the body, manipulated by touch and proprioception (Figure 3.1). Interestingly, critics of BIM in particular and digital design processes in general point to a postulated lack of a haptic design experience in these processes. If not touched by the human hand, presumably, there is something lacking in design. Yet try to use your favorite software application on another user's machine, perhaps with different tool layouts,

FIGURE 3.1 The author's two preferred drawing implements: below, a Hex-O-Matic Retro 1951 0.7 mm mechanical pencil, and an EM Workman 5.5 mm soft lead clutch lead holder, above. Both are mechanical lead pencils, and one would use them for very different drawings. Moreover, which pencil was selected would prejudice the nature of the drawing itself.

keyboard shortcuts, and preferences, or even operating systems. Notice how using even the most familiar software whose commands and gestures are second nature is suddenly almost painful. It's clear that even at the most basic, gestural level, there is a haptic quality to software use.

Too, there is a vague context around the word *tool*. We might first distinguish tools from *processes*. Processes involve the use of one or more tools over time in order to produce a desired result. A coherent process has an organizational logic and perhaps employs related tools. When we talk about a digital design process, we assume a predominance of digital tools (software and hardware), with means of converting any analog data (say, hand sketches) into a digital format such that it can be incorporated into said digital design process. Yet if we refer to a particular BIM software application as a whole—say, ARCHICAD—as a tool, we may also refer to specific software components within the application as tools, like a "wall tool" or a "stair tool". There may also be software tools—like Vectorworks' graphical scripting language, Marionette—that are as much like our definition of processes as they are like tools. So we have tools within processes within tools within processes, like recursive Russian dolls. Fundamentally, however, for the sake of our discussion, we needn't get pedantic over our definitions. If it's used in a task, we can safely shorthand it as a "tool" (Figure 3.2); a series of tasks I take to constitute a "process".

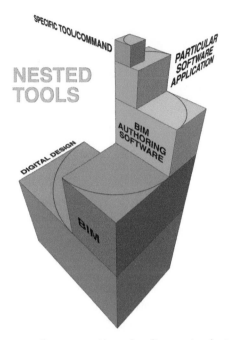

FIGURE 3.2 Stacked meanings, or the semantics of software tools: BIM is a tool, a particular BIM application is a tool, and the software itself contains individual functions or connected functions, all of which might be termed tools.

Some critics of BIM and digital design want it both ways: design is purely a function of the architect's talent, training, and skill (the heroic view of architects), and BIM dumbs down design. BIM supposedly does the latter in several ways:

□ It provides the user ready-made architectural components (wall types, columns, beams, floor and roof systems, windows and doors, etc.), developed by software engineers, that can facilely be dropped into the design without thoughtful consideration of the appropriateness of the component nor the project's design intent. The end result is a thoughtless box that deceptively looks more designed than it actually is. Moreover, BIM projects tend to all share a certain sameness and are easily identifiable (Figure 3.3).

□ By limiting the user to designing from a prescribed list of BIM objects, the designer's creativity is hampered. This is the problem of "When you have a hammer every (design) problem looks like a nail." Even when the menu of BIM objects and their richness increases with every passing year, this problem persists, merely becoming less obvious and more pernicious. In the end, the architect is not designing but assembling from a broad but prescribed kit of parts.

FIGURE 3.3 Do architectural projects whose design has been executed in BIM have a certain sameness that betrays their software of origin? Can you tell just by looking whether this project was designed and documented in a BIM process?

Image credit: Lévy Kohlhaas Architects.

- By excluding the haptic art of drawing from the design process, the architect is unable to engage those cognitive processes that are inherent and crucial to design.
- BIM software's failing to incorporate highly detailed element models excludes it from consideration as a medium for developing architectural details. When the BIM window is a coarsely simplified model of the real window for example, the architect cannot use it to legitimately explore detailed design. As a result, computer-aided design and drafting (CADD) techniques are still needed to execute a complete project.

As the reader might expect, I don't subscribe to these conclusions. Nevertheless, underlying these points are legitimate concerns that should be addressed with intellectual honesty and curiosity. Let's dig in and look at those points, and more importantly their relationship to the latent interests of designers.

BIM: What It Is and What It Isn't

BIM is a digital environment using data-rich, three-dimensional geometry to represent building systems. By "environment" I mean specialized computer software, the hardware on which it necessarily operates, and the activities undertaken within the software, as well as associated activities outside the software (i.e., interactions between people working together on a building project). "Data-rich" means that the components and systems of the building information model are not merely representing geometry, but contain user-attached and/or inherent data identifying salient characteristics. Data-less 3D models are not per

FIGURE 3.4 As compelling, attractive, or useful for qualitative design assessment, data-less models are not BIM. The "I" in BIM is a critical component, not only allowing appropriate and contextual sharing of models among BIM stakeholders, but also enabling quantitative design processes within BIM.

Model courtesy of Jeffrey Ouellette.

se BIM, though they might be used as part of an overall BIM workflow (Figure 3.4). There are additional features that may characterize BIM processes but are not essential to meet the strict definition.

BIM Often but Does Not Necessarily Involve Multiple Participants

For quite some time there has been a distinction between Big BIM and little bim: Building Information Modeling (the process), and the building information model (the digital artifact, or the software platform on which it is produced)—notably expressed by Finith Jernigan in his seminal 2007 book, *BIG BIM little bim* (4Site Press). The explicit distinction is that BIM is truly BIM when it allows multiple design stakeholders to collaborate by sharing data, ideally developing (a) federated building model(s), each design stakeholder contributing to the model(s) according to her professional discipline. BIM is not merely a software application, and one cannot simply use a particular software platform and expect to reap all the benefits of a BIM process.

One perhaps unintended implicit value of "big BIM" is that a sole practitioner intrinsically cannot be fully vested in BIM. If a building model falls in the forest, and only one person is there to design it, is it BIM? I embrace that BIM offers rich opportunities for sharing data and is a significant opportunity for integrated

FIGURE 3.5 For this project, the architect employed a BIM process and the structural engineer did not. Data was shared and exchanged in "flattened" 2D drawing formats, in this case DWG and PDF. In instances where structural members' dimensions and locations had a potential impact on the home's architecture, the architect modeled the structural steel based on the engineer's drawings. There are opportunities for error when such transcriptions are made, underscoring the benefits of end-to-end BIM. That notwithstanding, a BIM process is possible and beneficial even when only one design team member is employing it.

project delivery. I also acknowledge that BIM in solo or small practice can be legitimate. Moreover, the degree to which a design team integrates data can fall on a spectrum (Figure 3.5). The salient characteristic of BIM is its "I"—information—which, while implying and even strongly favoring data sharing, does not by any means require it.

BIM May Be Parametric

But it doesn't have to be. Parametric modeling is a powerful digital process by which elements of the geometry are dependent on parameters. These may be quantitative values, such as common building objects modeled by a built-in tool whose geometrical output responds to user numerical input. A straightforward example would be a parametric door object whose width, height, thickness, and so on are defined by the user's numerical inputs. The inputs and in some instances configuration options are limited by the software developer, and these types of tools offer a greater ease of use with the tradeoff of potentially not meeting certain niche needs. For example, if the software developer did not anticipate the need for barn-style door (leaf parallel to wall suspended on rollers operating on a wall-mounted rail), the user may not be able apply such a door without some workaround or developing a custom tool.

A more customized degree of parametrization involves the user establishing rules or relationships between two or more discrete geometries (Figure 3.6). A fairly simple case would be a steel plate whose bolt-hole pattern is related to the overall plate's geometry; as the plate is resized, the bolt holes move to accommodate the new geometry within the established rules (some configurations may "break" the rule and create an invalid result).

Finally, the greatest degree of parameterization is represented by the user's development of fully custom tools under the umbrella of the BIM authoring software. Graphical scripting languages such as Vectorworks' Marionette toolkit facilitate the development of such custom tools by those users who lack coding expertise.

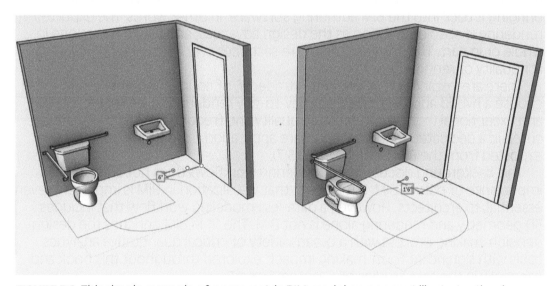

FIGURE 3.6 This simple example of a parametric BIM model component illustrates the dependencies of the linked geometries. Here, the dimension string is bound to the lavatory and the door, serving both to call out the distance between them and control it (left). As the dimension is modified, the geometry is correspondingly altered, moving the door along the wall to comply with accessibility requirements in this case (right). Such parametric dependencies can be quite complex, with a tendency to a correspondingly higher fragility when contradictory parameters cannot be resolved.

BIM Is Not Data-less Modeling

A significant attraction of BIM for architects and other visual designers is the ability to readily present a project in three dimensions. Moreover, with some contemporary BIM authoring software, a variety of rendering options ranging from the artistic to the photorealistic are built right in. Three-dimensional views may be projected orthogonally or in perspective, often with some form of vanishing point control for the latter. Sectional or clipped views are optional in some software. Such innate rendering capabilities allow and even encourage the close integration of visualization and presentation into the BIM workflow. Whereas early generations of authoring software offered a few limited presentation options (generally hidden line rendering and some form of basic surface rendering), integration of powerful rendering engines reduces or even eliminates the exporting of the BIM model to dedicated rendering software for all but the most demanding photo-rendering or animation tasks. Streamlining the presentation workflow, despite some rendering tradeoffs, means that renderings can be produced at any moment in the design's evolution, often in real time, allowing very rapid evaluation of qualitative design decisions. Moreover, once an exported model is rendered in separate software, there's no direct means of bringing it back into the BIM authoring software. In other words, the exported rendering is obsolete as soon as the design advances, and has to be redone in whole or in part. The designer therefore sacrifices efficiency of workflow (time) for quality of rendering.

There are instances that justify this tradeoff, of course. Too, the designer can choose a hybrid approach, whereby day-to-day renderings are executed in BIM, and exceptional (both in the sense of quality and frequency) renderings are executed in a dedicated rendering software application from a base 3D geometry exported from the BIM model (Figure 3.7).

This background discussion of rendering workflows does not address the importance of data in BIM. It is evident that visualization in BIM is important, even essential, to architects. However, a data-less modeling workflow that includes 3D geometry and rendering alone is not BIM. The "I" in BIM enriches the design decision-making process with a broad variety of critical quantitative analytics tools with significant form-making impact, explored throughout this book and especially in the case studies of Chapters 5 and 6:

- Architectural integration and expression of **passive environmental systems:** orientation, envelope typology and morphology, natural ventilation through wind-driven and stack effects, sun shading, daylighting, water collection for building hydrology.

- **Active environmental systems:** photovoltaics, solar thermal collection, artificial lighting.

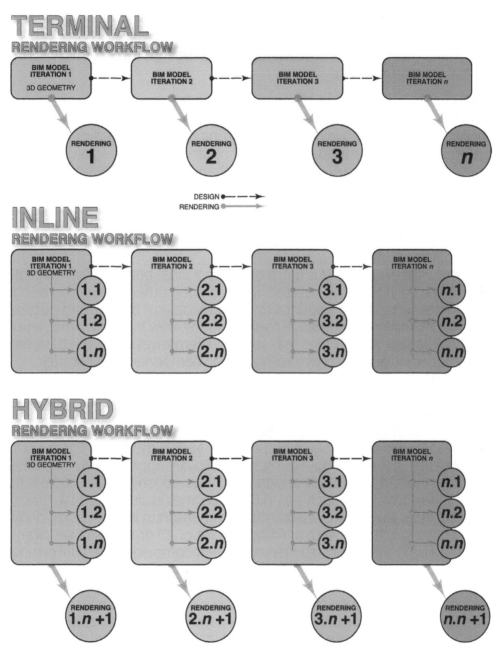

FIGURE 3.7 Diagram comparing a brachiated rendering/visualization workflow (above) with an integrated, iterative presentation workflow in a larger BIM context (middle). While the former may allow for marginally higher-quality renderings (conceptually represented here with heavier process lines), the integrated workflow facilitates more iterations by virtue of its ease and avoiding "terminal" renderings. For projects where highest- quality renderings are required, a hybrid approach (bottom) allows for faster, integrated "inline" renderings punctuated by occasional "terminal" visualization output.

- **Balancing competing agendas,** such as the tension between optimizing the architectural response to topography and solar optimization.
- Use of BIM geometrical and property data for **design informed by structure** and constructibility.

The dominant narrative of BIM as a platform for capitalizing on documentation efficiencies and error reduction has fostered an attitude that tends to overlook these quantitative design opportunities. Design studios that employ BIM merely as a standardized modeling application with the sole objective of improving production efficiency and enhanced clash detection miss out on the possibility of informing the design itself, perhaps even taking it in new directions altogether. This is not to dismiss BIM's efficiency; it is in a real sense the enabling technology that makes deeper design processes possible. Without the inherent production value of BIM, computational design might be time prohibitive.

That notwithstanding, BIM is more than just "faster, better CADD." Capitalizing on BIM data in the ways bulleted above, among others, can reveal design opportunities and suggest solutions to design problems theretofore outside the designer's thinking. Alternative configurations, new building forms, and even entire architectural vocabularies may suggest themselves when the designer includes quantitative analysis as a key validation component in a broader qualitative design process.

Moreover, a 3D yet BIM-less workflow is both inefficient and represents missed design opportunities. It's regrettably common for firms to develop geometry-only 3D models in early design phases, making extensive use of data-less modeling applications, whether surface or NURBS modelers. There's nothing wrong with BIM-less modeling—using such software appropriately can fulfill an important role in a practice's design workflow—so long as the model is not fetishized. However, when such a workflow becomes exclusive of BIM, then the design process is limited with a potential commensurate loss of design depth. Simply exporting a 3D model to a "flattened" set of 2D drawings to be taken up in CADD and brought to construction document completion is an unfortunately all-too common workflow (Figure 3.8). Moreover, having 3D "design" distinct from 2D "documentation" establishes a definitive demarcation that is artificial and encourages a hierarchy of designers versus drafters. This harkens back to old models of practice organization, wherein the designers occupied offices at the periphery of the space while production staff filled a central drafting pool. A bit out of date.

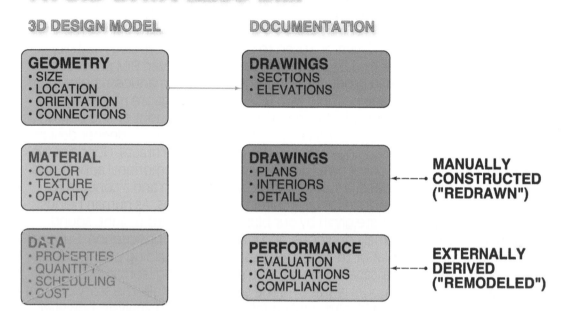

FIGURE 3.8 Inefficient and a missed opportunity: workflows that implement CADD or even BIM superficially once the design is fully developed in a 3D modeling application. Much or most of the design must be redrawn, and any performance or compliance calculations must be constructed outside the design model, requiring additional work and introducing the strong possibility of inconsistent or wrong information.

BIM Is Data

In a real sense, it would be a false paradigm to consider that BIM equals (a) model(s) plus data. The model *is* the data, or, more accurately, part of it. The geometry of the model's components—their location, orientation, extents in three dimensions, topography, surface area, and volume—are part of the data of the comprehensive building model. And BIM comprises geometry that is both **intelligent** and **semantic.** Intelligent in that it potentially has data attached to it beyond that of its geometrical definition. A steel structural member could thus include data for its density (in order to calculate mass and therefore structural properties or cost). The geometry is semantic in that it has meaning and therefore context. That steel member may be also tagged as a beam or a column, fulfilling a structural function or not (i.e., distinguished as a "structural" or "architectural" element), and those distinctions would affect statics calculations performed with BIM structural analysis software.

The intelligence and semanticism of BIM is a highly significant concept. Those digital models that lack either intelligence (data) or semantic distinctions of building elements cannot be readily analyzed. Such models may have components merely classed or layered by typology strictly out of a concern for their graphical representation, just as DWG layers are used to control object typology visibility and line weight. While that may be important to CADD and even BIM production workflows, BIM is more than production. Intelligence and semanticism point to an underlying proposition made possible with BIM: that buildings are more than discrete collections of arbitrary objects, and instead can be thought of and behave as *systems.* A "systems thinking" approach to architecture requires a deeper design sensitivity that considers buildings as more than sculptural artifacts. Nor does systems thinking preclude architecture for sensory response, emotional appeal, and dare I say even beauty. Indeed, a systems approach to design and a concern for performance may only enhance those architectural concerns. As human beings, our responses to buildings are given by our biological reactions to light, sound, and skin response to thermal conditions, and inform our proprioception. Building performance touches on all of these issues; designing for building performance increases our architectural satisfaction rather than detracting from it.

A three-dimensional model is static, in the sense that it tells the story of what the building looks like in an idealized moment. Add data and analysis, however, and that model becomes open to simulation: testing its performance over a variety of conditions or over time, in fairly straightforward or complex ways. For example, numerous energy analysis tools are available, either built into BIM authoring software or accessible by exporting data-rich BIM models to dedicated energy analysis software using formats like gbXML (Green Building eXtensible Markup Language) or IFC (Industry Foundation Classes), to name two. Energy analysis in particular requires simulation over time, as climate generally and seasonal changes particularly affect building thermal and energy performance. Full energy modeling iterates a year's worth of average climate data for a given location in order to determine external energy loads. For energy modeling, building geometry is modeled in a simplified form, so walls may be represented by a plane or windows by a rectangular surface without granular articulation. The data attached to those simplified surfaces are key: wall orientation, reflectance, emissivity, and thermal resistance are all accounted for. Similarly, window thermal properties are based on the overall window assembly, so it's not necessary to differentiate individual components like jambs, sashes, and glazing: the window as a whole has data attached to it representing its VT (visual transmittance), SHGC (solar heat gain coefficient), and U-factor (thermal conductance). Occupancy of interior spaces is critical, defining the uses of rooms and their corresponding energy loads and schedules. Space objects thus become critical to energy modeling software, even though they are abstractions that do not represent building components at all—they represent volumes of air and activities (Figure 3.9).

FIGURE 3.9 BIM for simulation. For energy modeling or simulation, the geometry of the BIM model is simplified and extraneous components that have negligible impact on energy performance are excluded, while abstract data for occupancy and activities must also be considered in the simulation.

On a simpler level, SimTread is a BIM software plugin thatsimulates pedestrian egress patterns to help designers analyze and improvetraffic patterns for events, evacuation, and emergency preparedness. Although atwo-dimensional simulation, pedestrian "agents" recognize barriers like walls,have variable rates of motion, and can exit through doors at realistic rates.

BIM Is Not Just a File Format

I've often heard architects or their staff say something like "I'll get you the CADD file," or "We have the project in CADD." What they meant, of course, was AutoDesk's AutoCAD. The presumption was that CADD and AutoCAD are interchangeable, which is hardly the case. AutoCAD is assuredly CADD, but not all CADD is AutoCAD. But there were and are numerous other legitimate CADD platforms, many without "CAD" in their names. When someone offers to send you "the CADD file" what they likely mean is a DWG—the proprietary format of AutoCAD files. So prevalent was DWG as a requirement for interoperability in the 1980s and 1990s that other software vendors banded together and reverse engineered the format in order to develop file importing and exporting libraries, and thus was born the OpenDWG Alliance, now the Open Design Alliance.

Nowadays, there's a parallel conflation of BIM and AutoDesk's Revit, though the error is more profound. First, Revit is a BIM-authoring platform, and the BIM ecosystem is far broader and encompasses other applications than those for authoring architectural, structural, mechanical, or civil engineering content (Figure 3.10).

AUTHORING / DESIGN

ARCHITECTURAL

4M IDEA Architecture
AutoCAD Architecture
ViCADo.arc
NTItools Arkitekt (Revit plug-ins)
cadwork wood
Vectorworks Architect
Digital Project
ARCHICAD
Allplan Architecture
VisualARQ
DDS-CAD Architect
Bentley speedikon V8i (SELECTseries4)
Revit Architecture
IFC-to-RDF Web Service
SPIRIT
EliteCAD AR
4MCAD PRO
Edificius
AutoScheme
Renga Architecture
AECOsim Building Designer V8i
BricsCAD
ARCHLine.XP

BUILDING SERVICES

GALA Construction Software
DProfiler
IFC Takeoff for Microsoft Excell
Synchro Professional
CostOS BIM Estimating
BIMProject evolution
DDS-CAD Construction
Navisworks
ISY Calcus
Vico Office Suite
CostX
SUperPlan
Tekla BIMsight
EcoDomus PM
AutoBid SheetMetal
SmartKalk
PriMus-IFC
Asta Powerproject BIM
Cubicost TAS
RIB iTWO
CerTus-PN
ArtrA
CerTus-IFC
ManTus-IFC
usBIM.gantt
usBIM.platform

STRUCTURAL

SteelVis
Advance Concrete
NTItools Konstruksjon (Revit plug-ins)
Tilt-Werks
AVEVA Boca Steel
Revit Structure
Advance Design
Allplan Engineering
Tekla Structures
Advance Steel
StruCad
SDS/2
RSTAB
CSiBridge
4M STRAD
FEM-Design
AxisVM
STRAKON
InfoCAD
SPACE GASS
Bentley Structural Modeler v8i
SOFiSTiK Structural Desktop (SSD)
ViCADo.ing
ScaleCAD
SAP2000
Scia Engineer
ETABS
RFEM
CAD/QST
Tricalc
CYPECAD
SAFI 3D
EdiLus
AECOsim Building Designer V8i

GENERAL MODELING

Ziggurat
Constructivity Model Editor
ggRhinoIFC
SolidWorks Premium
FreeCAD
usBIM.clash
usBIM.code
Solid Edge
SketchUp

FIGURE 3.10 The ecosphere of current BIM applications. Only a portion of these are authoring applications, and of those Revit (in all of its various professional forms) is but one of many.

COORDINATION

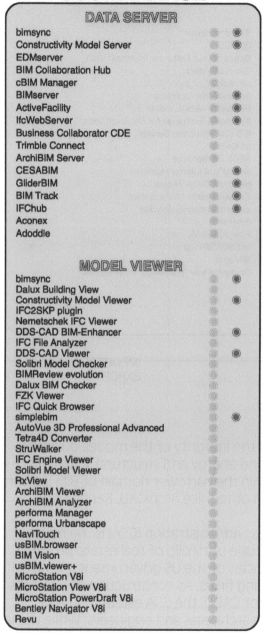

DATA SERVER

- bimsync
- Constructivity Model Server
- EDMserver
- BIM Collaboration Hub
- cBIM Manager
- BIMserver
- ActiveFacility
- IfcWebServer
- Business Collaborator CDE
- Trimble Connect
- ArchiBIM Server
- CESABIM
- GliderBIM
- BIM Track
- IFChub
- Aconex
- Adoddle

MODEL VIEWER

- bimsync
- Dalux Building View
- Constructivity Model Viewer
- IFC2SKP plugin
- Nemetschek IFC Viewer
- DDS-CAD BIM-Enhancer
- IFC File Analyzer
- DDS-CAD Viewer
- Solibri Model Checker
- BIMReview evolution
- Dalux BIM Checker
- FZK Viewer
- IFC Quick Browser
- simplebim
- AutoVue 3D Professional Advanced
- Tetra4D Converter
- StruWalker
- IFC Engine Viewer
- Solibri Model Viewer
- RxView
- ArchiBIM Viewer
- ArchiBIM Analyzer
- performa Manager
- performa Urbanscape
- NaviTouch
- usBIM.browser
- BIM Vision
- usBIM.viewer+
- MicroStation V8i
- MicroStation View V8i
- MicroStation PowerDraft V8i
- Bentley Navigator V8i
- Revu

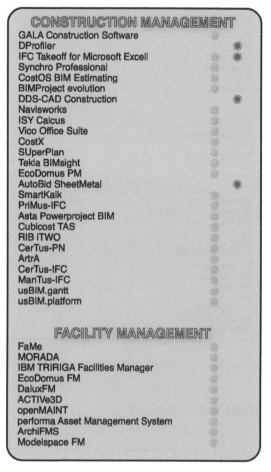

CONSTRUCTION MANAGEMENT

- GALA Construction Software
- DProfiler
- IFC Takeoff for Microsoft Excell
- Synchro Professional
- CostOS BIM Estimating
- BIMProject evolution
- DDS-CAD Construction
- Navisworks
- ISY Calcus
- Vico Office Suite
- CostX
- SUperPlan
- Tekla BIMsight
- EcoDomus PM
- AutoBid SheetMetal
- SmartKalk
- PriMus-IFC
- Asta Powerproject BIM
- Cubicost TAS
- RIB iTWO
- CerTus-PN
- ArtrA
- CerTus-IFC
- ManTus-IFC
- usBIM.gantt
- usBIM.platform

FACILITY MANAGEMENT

- FaMe
- MORADA
- IBM TRIRIGA Facilities Manager
- EcoDomus FM
- DaluxFM
- ACTIVe3D
- openMAINT
- performa Asset Management System
- ArchiFMS
- Modelspace FM

FIGURE 3.10 (Continued)

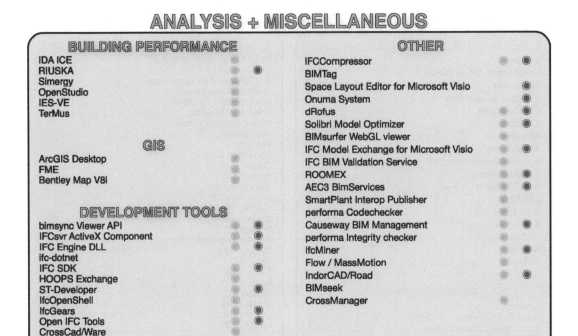

FIGURE 3.10 *(Continued)*

BIM software includes checkers to validate the integrity of the model, quantity surveying software for detailed takeoffs, and energy and structural analysis software, among others (Figure 3.11). Even within the narrower domain of BIM authoring software, Revit faces competition from others like ArchiCAD, Bentley, and Vectorworks, among others.

In the United States, the General Services Administration (GSA) is the nation's largest landlord, owning and managing a huge portfolio of real estate properties that it leases out to the various agencies of the US government. As such, it hires countless architectural and engineering firms. As construction documents became digital with widespread adoption of CADD, the GSA established and evolved its requirements to its contracting architects and engineers. While those submission standards and protocols were not requirements for those firms not employed by the GSA, as the country's largest landlord it has a significant influence on the entire industry, extending even to those practices that did not do government work. In previous decades the GSA came to insist that

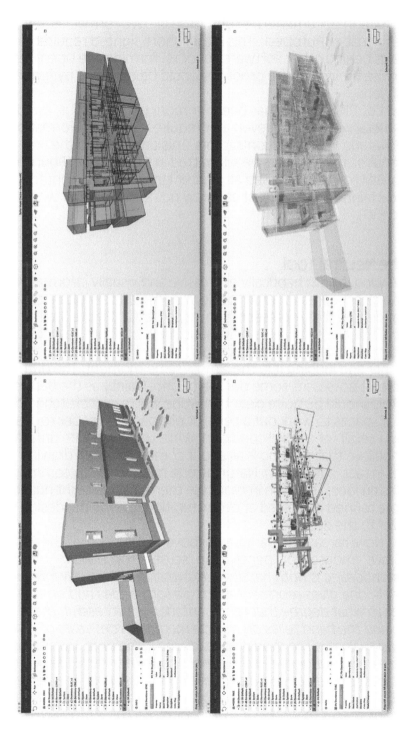

FIGURE 3.11 A project model originated in one BIM-authoring software application and viewed in a model checker. Interoperability is a key ingredient of BIM. East Dormitory Project data files by Prairie Sky Consulting are available at https://www.prairieskyconsulting.com/testing.htm. Files used by permission under Attribution-ShareAlike 4.0 International license.

completed construction documents be submitted in DWG format (as .dwg files), a proprietary file format of AutoDesk. This rather short-sighted requirement was part of the impetus behind other software vendors' forming the Open Design Alliance, as otherwise their software products would be unusable by firms doing any government work.

With the advent of BIM, the GSA has been far more perspicacious, avoiding stipulating a proprietary BIM format even as it requires building information modeling workflows and files of its contractors. This time around the administration requires that projects be submitted in IFC (Industry Foundation Classes), a neutral BIM format discussed at greater length in the Chapter 2. So while Revit is certainly BIM, BIM is just as surely not Revit. In other words, BIM is not spelled RVT.

The Myth of the Neutral Tool

I contend that drawing is both haptically expressive and visually informative. As one draws, one gives representation to a formal idea and simultaneously evaluates to what degree that representation is successful (Figure 3.12). There is tactile feedback, and the hand relies on muscle memory from years of prac-tice. One expresses and evaluates the drawing at nearly the same time, commit-ting an idea to paper and judging it in the almost same moment. The outcome is unknown or at least possesses some degree of uncertainty as the designer begins to draw. This should be quite clear to anyone who's ever sketched out a bubble diagram of spaces to work out a parti, or put pencil to paper to sketch out a construction detail for a novel condition. While those who are unfamiliar with design may believe that drawing is all about communication, drawing (in the design process) is in fact *exploration*. Naturally one might draw to communicate an established design idea, and even in that case there may be slight nuances to the design that are refined or altered at every iteration, even if the design solu-tion seems familiar to the designer.

Do you agree? Now, reread the paragraph above and substitute the verb "to model" for "to draw," "mouse" for "pencil," and "screen" for "paper":

I contend that modeling is both haptically expressive and visually informa-tive. As one models, one gives representation to a formal idea and simulta-neously evaluates to what degree that representation is successful. There is tactile feedback, and the hand relies on muscle memory from years of practice. One expresses and evaluates the model at nearly the same time, committing an idea to the screen and judging it in the almost same moment. The outcome is unknown or at least possesses some degree of uncertainty as the designer begins to model. This should be quite clear to anyone who's ever sketched out a bubble diagram of spaces to work out a parti, or picked up a mouse to sketch

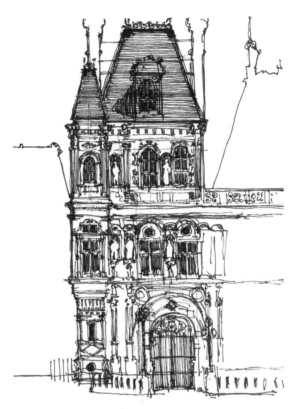

FIGURE 3.12 A hand-drawn study of a portion of the Hôtel de Ville in Paris. When in the field, notice how you think you know a building by looking at it, until you start to draw it. You may only then realize that what you thought you saw actually isn't quite how the building is. It is by the act of drawing it that you really see it.

out a construction detail for a novel condition. While those who are unfamiliar with design may believe that modeling is all about communication, modeling (in the design process) is in fact exploration. Naturally one might model to communicate an established design idea, and even in that case there may be slight nuances to the design that are refined or altered at every iteration, even if the design solution seems familiar to the designer.

I wrote the above variation of the previous paragraph as an argument for the haptic legitimacy of modeling, for those who cling to notion that the pencil is the preeminent design tool. I happen to keep my pencil with me always, and I'm quite fond of it. I'm also clear that I could never touch it again and be no less an architect for it. So much for the illegitimacy of digital modeling as an exploratory medium of design.

The above comparison of pencil and paper on the one hand and mouse and computer on the other is an analogy restricted to gestural interfaces, and barely touches on the cognitive processes beneath the respective design methodologies. For the sake of argument, let's take the case that pencils and mice have equivalent design legitimacy. If they were merely a matter of personal preference, there wouldn't be much of a debate. Skeptics and protagonists of digital design get positional about approaches because of the value they ascribe to their design processes, and/or they devalue and perhaps even hold the other in contempt.

One inconsistency is that advocates of analog design processes simultaneously hold that design tools are neutral—that is, that the ability to design resides in the designer, not her tool. While it's clear that a tool is the repository of design, by virtue of being a tool it facilitates a particular activity. The contradiction occurs when analog designers then claim that digital design leads to inferior design outcomes. Yet if the tool were truly neutral, how could this be the case?

There is actually a deeper question to consider, beyond one of haptic processes: Is there such a thing as a neutral tool? Does the use of one particular tool or design process over another lead to particular architectural conclusions? Does the tool influence or even prejudice the design? It's not clear to me whether this question can be objectively and definitively answered, and it's nevertheless useful as the beginning of a valuable inquiry.

It seems clear that what influence a tool has is dependent on the author's relationship to it. To make the point, consider two hypothetical designers of equivalent professional experience, each using the same BIM authoring software. One uses BIM strictly for 3D visualization and to improve efficiency of the production of design and documentation drawings. We might call that kind of workflow "BiM," with a little i. Information may be collated, extracted, indexed, presented, and referenced, but it isn't used as an exploratory medium. The data is never made to answer the designer's question of "What if . . . ?" Maybe a drawing index is automatically generated from the deliverable sheets, drawings and details are cross-referenced such that the drawing set is internally coordinated, or door and window schedules are generated from the model. There's obviously value to all that, and software programmers and developers have spent a great deal of effort in making this kind of bread-and-butter production efficiency as solid and seamless as they can. But that's it. While the data inherent to BIM is put to some use, it's limited to *expressing what the designer already knows about the design*.

Now take the case of another designer who is using the same software. Only this designer considers the model's data as valid an opportunity to design as the model's appearance. The model is not only used for 3D visualization and efficient production, but it is *queried*. Perhaps the total envelope surface area is compared to the floor area, or south-facing glass is compared to internal exposed thermal mass, or the size of opposite exterior operable openings are compared to calculate rate of wind-driven air flow for natural ventilation. Any number of questions can be asked of the model, just as the case studies in Chapters 5 and 6 suggest. And obviously the designer is required to have a certain level of expertise to ask the appropriate questions, and to be able to meaningfully interpret the responses. It's likely not the case that the designer is fumbling in the dark, and of course the question can prejudice the response. But what is key is that this designer is asking the design to *reveal something about itself that wasn't already known*.

Guiding Principles

Expanding the use of BIM into the practice of design is a large undertaking, full of technical, social, and professional challenges. There are a handful of helpful guiding principles to keep in mind. While perhaps introspective, they are not intended as nor do they constitute a coherent philosophy of design. Rather, these are empirically derived principles observed through years of practice.

Precision Is Not Accuracy

Given the highly detailed level of information available in BIM, it's an understandable pitfall to mistake very granular information for veracity. In fact, precision and accuracy are two different phenomena. *Precision* is the degree to which a value or calculation is exact, and it is commonly associated with accuracy. However, it's possible to have very exact numbers that are completely wrong. *Accuracy* is a measure of correctness. An approximation by itself cannot be absolutely accurate, but given the choice between an accurate but imprecise value and a precise but inaccurate one, the former is obviously desirable. Even a stopped clock is right twice a day.

In early design, it's possible, but probably not useful, to be precise. For one thing, whatever is being measured is likely to change—perhaps only a little—so measurements to three decimal places may be misleadingly authoritative. For example, for many projects we engage in early design *energy analysis*, meaning that building systems and components are assessed using well-established design guidelines and rules for performance. The goal of analysis is not to predict actual performance, but to guide the designer in making relative design decisions, e.g., "Wall A has a 5% better thermal performance than wall B" (Figure 3.13). *Energy modeling,* on the other hand, uses physics modeling (typically based on FEA, finite element analysis) to simulate building performance with greater certainty and detail. Unfortunately, while it is pretty *precise*, in

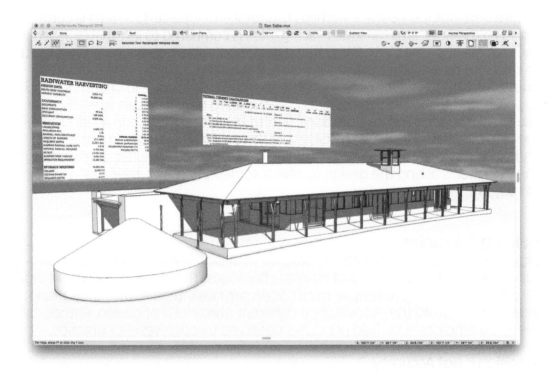

FIGURE 3.13 An approximate but reasonable value for a building performance report is preferable to a highly precise but wildly wrong one. Early performance analysis based on early design phases when all givens about the project are not yet known can still yield very useful design information.

order to be *accurate* energy modeling generally requires a wide range of project data—from the exact mechanical systems employed to lighting to occupant schedules—that may be not known at schematic design. Moreover, by the time the model is mature enough to appropriately employ energy modeling, many of the design decisions have been made. Hence, it's critical that less granular energy analysis methodologies be used early in the design, when less is known about the project but more is subject to evolution. Finally, it should be noted that even energy modeling often does not accurately predict real-world performance. This is not because the computer models are poor or the physics are not well understood. Rather, buildings are inhabited by people, who tend to make chaotic and unpredictable operational choices.

Make Your Own Tools

Most BIM authoring software allows a certain degree of tool customization in the form of scripting. As Rhino Grasshopper, a graphical scripting language, has grown in popularity among designers and architecture students, BIM application developers have taken note (while a very robust 3D modeler and potentially a component in an overall BIM workflow, Rhino is not a BIM application per se). Revit has Dynamo and Vectorworks has Marionette, for example; these types of visual programming tools are discussed in greater depth elsewhere (Chapters 1 and 7). Even aside from these, most BIM authoring software allows for a great deal of flexibility and customization (Figure 3.14). On the modeling side, custom model elements can be created, standardized, and deployed (these are sometimes called *families* or *symbols*). For data, reports or worksheets are like embedded spreadsheets and can query model elements and report them in a form that is readily made into an informational tool with no more programming knowledge than would be required to create an Excel spreadsheet. Many of my sustainable design tools for Vectorworks are simply worksheets, querying the model for projected roof area to recommend the size of a rainwater harvesting cistern, or using designated doors and windows as air inlets and outlets to calculate the air flow rate for a passive thermal chimney.

Such customization, whether simple spreadsheets or more complex scripts, allow the user to create or adapt their own tools when the software developer doesn't have an off-the-shelf solution for a particular need (Figure 3.15). While they require some work to create up front, they quickly become an effective investment in time as they are reused project after project, or even adapted further for slightly different project needs. Simple or sophisticated, custom

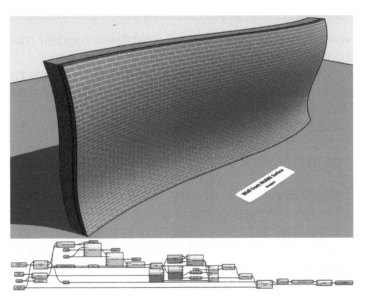

FIGURE 3.14 An example of a graphical script and the corresponding 3D geometry it controls. Such scripts can also be used for nonmodeling tasks like custom graphics or file organization utilities.

Image courtesy of Vectorworks, Inc.

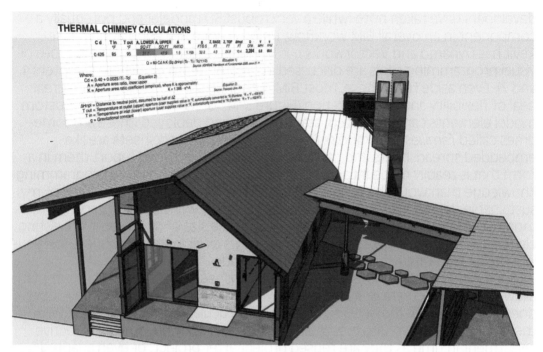

FIGURE 3.15 A worksheet with model inputs can be a powerful custom design tool, even if relatively simple. Here air inlets and outlet sizes and their relative heights populate a worksheet to calculate approximate thermal chimney air flow rates due to the stack effect.

tools required for a particular process have a relatively modest threshold to deploy, and potentially a very high yield.

"What is not proscribed is required" was a motto of a science tutor I had at St. John's College in Santa Fe, New Mexico (where faculty are called tutors, not professors). As a molecular biophysicist, Dr. Gerald Myers was instrumental in creating a database of HIV genetic sequences in the mid-1980s. As a teacher, he urged his students to be inquisitive, curious, and open minded. I interpreted his dictum to suggest that exploration and inquiry were mandatory for a scientist or researcher, and that anything that didn't contradict known laws was not only fair game but compulsory. Just as with the sciences, design is an exploration of what could be true. Here architectural solutions rather than physical laws are being uncovered, but the discovery of something unknown is nevertheless the process and the goal. The designer who expresses something already known to her is polemicizing, not designing. As designers, we are called to always discover, explore, investigate, research, and create.

Data Is My Pencil, and It Can Be One of Yours Too

Obviously, there's a certain level of mastery required to be able to use BIM as a true design medium, and that competence lies in two distinct domains. The designer has to have a minimum level of expertise in using her software to be able to create meaningful reports. Given the wealth of software documentation and YouTube videos for most software, the barrier to entry is not technical but a willingness to expand proficiency with the tool, and time. And in addition, some design background must be present in order to know which investigations might yield meaningful or interesting results. Here half of what is required is what the designer probably already has: experience designing. In other words, enough experience in the design process generally to be able to formulate good questions. The other half of asking good questions is having the self-confidence to not know the answer.

Ironically, the most liberating thing about confidence is that it gives the designer room to fail. Self-doubt pulls the designer away from the ledge of discovery and into the safety—and darkness—of the cave. A fruitful investigation requires that the designer be willing to be surprised, be comfortable being uncomfortable, be vulnerable rather than arrogant, and be curious even if it seems the answer is obvious. The ingredients of BIM for design are the ingredients of all good design: confidence, curiosity, and surprise.

Chapter 4

Appropriate Technology

In our modern society we have a love-hate relationship with technology. On the one hand, we're enduringly optimistic, convinced that this new device or that new software package will transform our lives, banish all problems, and lead us into a shiny new future of exponential productivity growth and joyful, carefree work. On the other hand, we hate being shackled to our personal devices, having our time absorbed by managing our software and destroyed by hardware crashes, and spending all our energies dealing with bugs, software design shortcomings, and a bewildering ecosystem of software applications.

Just as with our human relationships, the problem with our relationship to technology lies in no small degree with largely unexamined and wholly unrealistic expectations, unencumbered by any sense of personal responsibility. We expect that software intended to assist in the design and construction of a complex building—a system of systems—will be able to anticipate all of our design needs while never getting in our way. Mind you, this building we're designing is imaginary (as it doesn't exist yet), and at least at the beginning of the design process we may not really be sure what it will even look like. Finally, we expect that regardless of the complexity of the design, the software will be simple and intuitive to use. In short, we want to be able to design the Sagrada Familia using Pac-Man.

So what are realistic expectations for our use of BIM? What questions should users be asking of themselves about the appropriateness of technology? How does the technology of BIM fit into a larger perspective of the nature of design and architecture?

Introduction

Initially the adoption of BIM among architects was a function of outside pressure from elsewhere in the AEC industry. Large contractors saw the benefits of BIM in calculating accurate quantity surveys and material takeoffs, identifying instances of failed coordination between trades or disciplines (clash detection), and optimizing construction sequencing (so-called 4D BIM). I've spoken with general contractors (GCs) who were so certain of BIM's benefits that they would routinely create BIM models from architects' 2D drawing sets; a digital model was worth the effort of creating "from scratch." I have even heard from GCs that they build their own, distinct BIM models even when the design team shares theirs—which would seem to undermine the value of shared, collaborative model.

Owners liked BIM in principle if contractors could deliver a project faster and with fewer errors at the same or lower cost. What's not to like? For architects, however, BIM adoption was slower to an even greater degree than CADD had been before it. Many architects were suspicious of new requirements from building owners that deliverables be in a BIM format. It wasn't clear (even to clients) what that meant exactly. To the skeptic, BIM meant more work and the potential for greater liability, all for the same fee. While social mechanisms like new architectural service agreements and insurance contracts have made strides in addressing these concerns, they have historically lagged behind the technology. Moreover, the architectural profession did not seek out BIM; architects for the most part were induced or required by other stakeholders to adopt it. Perhaps since architectural training had for centuries taught our profession to visualize spaces and three-dimensional assemblies from two-dimensional drawings, architects concluded that a 3D workflow was superfluous. Few architects felt that they needed a new way to go about designing and documenting buildings.

Figure 4.1 summarizes the three design workflows of manual drawing and modeling, CADD drawing coupled with manual modeling, and BIM; Figure 4.2 shows how those workflows share information among professionals.

Manual drafting requires both manual production and coordination; "data" (drawings) are created (drawn) and then recreated (redrawn), with perhaps some "automated" transfer thanks to tracing. If drawing creation is slow, editing is hardly faster. The computer may be a good content creation tool, but it shines as an editing tool, and CADD allows for more automated forward migration of data. That forward migration quickly breaks down when the medium changes. For example, when transitioning from hand-rendered concept sketches to drafted schematic design drawings, or when constructing foam core concept models from drafted drawings, everything has to be redone. Even so, models are disassociated from the drawings they represent (and vice versa). The model becomes a fly caught in amber, a snapshot in time of the evolution of the design, and a "dead end" in workflow terms, as it cannot be directly poured back into the drawing set. (Although admittedly I have known architects who include photos of concept models in their construction document sets, as a clever kind of primitive analog BIM). Presentation models are reduced to a kind of marketing; very useful to communicate or convince, but less useful to the architect as a critical tool. By then, most of the key design decisions have been made and, if not set in stone, at least laboriously cut in bass wood and museum board.

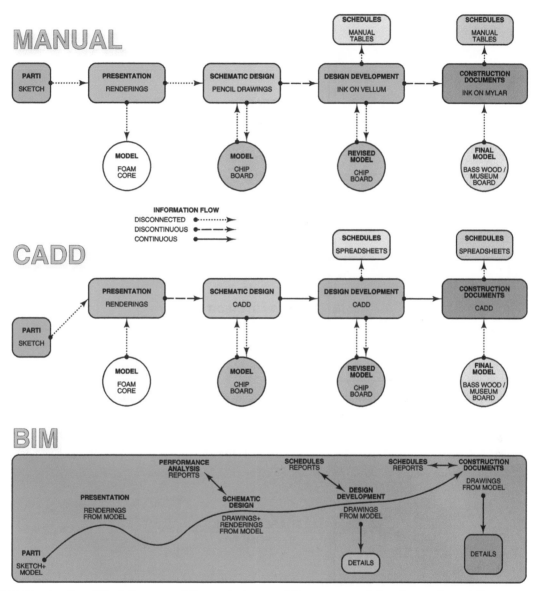

FIGURE 4.1 Simplified diagram of three design workflows: manual drawing and modeling; CADD drafting and manual modeling; and BIM.

MANUAL

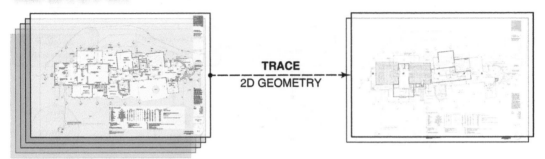

TRACE
2D GEOMETRY

CADD

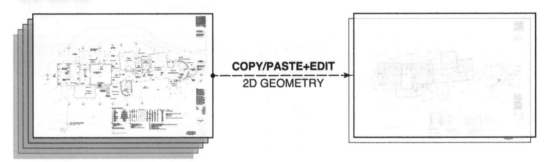

COPY/PASTE+EDIT
2D GEOMETRY

BIM

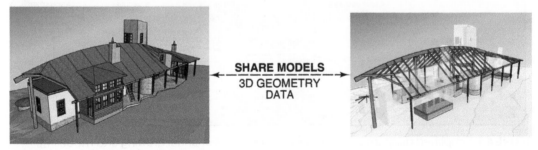

SHARE MODELS
3D GEOMETRY
DATA

FIGURE 4.2 The three workflows from Figure 4.1, and how they share information among design professionals.

Transitioning to BIM

Most large firms have already or plan to transition to BIM. According to the 2016 American Institute of Architects (AIA) Firm Survey, "larger firms have a . . . trend where adoption has been faster than expected. Only 2% report they have no plans to use BIM in 2015, compared to 10% in 2013." I have been lecturing for years at various professional conventions on the merits of BIM for small firms and for residential architecture. My previous book, *BIM in Small-Scale Sustainable Design*, was expressly aimed at the types of projects, residential and otherwise, that small firms execute. Yet the same AIA report shows 28% BIM adoption in small architecture firms in both 2013 and 2015:

> There remains a consistent percentage that does not plan to use BIM. The largest share of these, at 45%, are in small firms (under 10 employees). This is likely related to the high percentage of residential, given that 44% of firms with a residential specialization also report having no plans to use it . . . this percentage has remained relatively consistent.

While small firms have unique challenges to adopting BIM, a building information modeling workflow is as much a benefit to their projects as it is for large firms, although perhaps in different ways. BIM has been adopted in large firms and for large projects so prevalently because its coordination and interoperability advantages are so obvious. Buildings have became far more complex; Ramsey and Sleeper's 1932 first edition of *Architectural Graphic Standards* does not list "air conditioning" nor "mechanical" in the index, and there are only a total of six entries for anything electrical, and a dozen for plumbing (see Figure 4.3). Given the complicated nature of modern buildings, architects have a far greater burden of coordination, and BIM is well suited to address that. Moreover, owners of large buildings have come to see the operational value of having a digital model of their building, even if they don't always put it to best use.

For small firms, with fewer design stakeholders and somewhat more straight-forward coordination issues, BIM's interoperability is less alluring. Many small building owners don't know that BIM exists, even if they are vaguely aware that some architects model in 3D digitally. Yet BIM's advantages for small firms, underscored throughout this and my previous book, are nevertheless highly compelling:

□ Coordination within the drawing set (documentation)

□ Visualization (qualitative analysis)

□ Interoperability with other design professionals (coordination)

□ Quantitative analysis (the "I" in BIM)

□ Continuous, workflow-oriented, recursive design processes (iteration)

ARCHITECTURAL GRAPHIC STANDARDS
1932   2016

FIGURE 4.3 Facsimile excerpts from the index of the 1932 Architectural Graphic Standards with MEP topics compared to those from the 12th edition (2016).

Index content courtesy of John Wiley & Sons.

The first and third are the same benefits that accrue to large firm adoption of BIM. Documentation advantages are the "gateway" that might attract firms, large and small, to BIM, but that is only the tip of the iceberg (see Figure 4.4).

There are several strategies and tactics that a firm may consider in order to make a successful transition to a true BIM workflow. Newcomers to BIM should understand that transitioning to BIM is much more than just changing software platforms. As other portions of this book hopefully make abundantly clear, when fully implemented, BIM is a new way of designing that can have a profound effect on a practice.

But the costs of new software, hardware, and, less obviously, training required to implement BIM are not insignificant. Consider, however, that most firms upgrade software and hardware periodically, even when maintaining

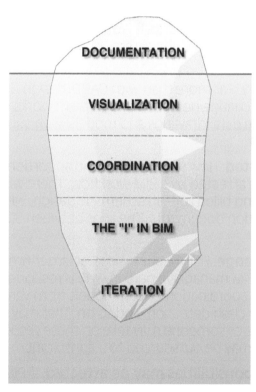

FIGURE 4.4 The BIM benefit "iceberg" for small firms. Iterative design—a continuous workflow process where the designer can readily loop back to earlier design decisions and advance them forward with minimal interruption—is the least obvious but most profound impact of BIM.

the same 2D workflow. Moreover, today's "prosumer" computers make for approachable, cost-effective, and surprisingly capable workstations. By timing a transition to BIM as these upgrades are scheduled, initial costs can be mitigated somewhat.

First Things First: Make a Firm Commitment to BIM

It may be obvious, but the first step to transitioning to BIM is to make a firm (pun intended) commitment to transitioning to BIM. This decision should not be taken lightly, and all concerned should recognize that it will impact almost all aspects of your architectural practice:

- **BIM will impact the design process**, from conceptual design, through design development, construction documents, and the construction phase. There will be far greater opportunities to mine and manipulate building data to make quantitatively informed design decisions. 3D visualization will permeate your design process, from early presentations to clients, to internal design meetings, and even in developing custom details. Your firm will create more rendering and animations. You may need to vigilantly stay on top of the graphic quality of your construction documents.

- **Collaboration is key.** Far more than with CADD, design documents are inter-related, and BIM will change how your design team works together, as well as how it may exchange data (drawings and models) with subconsultants and other design professionals.

- **Fees may be affected.** How you establish and apportion architectural design fees will probably be affected by a BIM workflow. There will likely be more work to be done—and billed for—in schematic design, with greater efficiencies in construction documents. The lines between SD, DD, and CDs will become blurrier.

- **Personnel may change.** For medium-sized or larger firms and projects, it's common to have a BIM manager, a person who is responsible for scheduling and maintaining the coordination of BIM models from various design stakeholders, performing clash detection, and so on. That may become a full-time position in your firm, or someone may take on these responsibilities as part of their portfolio, or it may be outsourced to a consultant.

- **Contracts and responsibilities may be affected.** If BIM deliverables become part of your services, you may need to adjust your service agreements. In our firm, the vast majority of our clients have little interest in the BIM data once the project is complete, so we rarely include the model itself as a deliverable.

Instead, we provide fairly traditional construction documents as our instruments of service, both to paper and PDF. Some clients may request or require a BIM model at project's end, and the cost and liability implications of that will obviously need to be addressed. AIA exhibit E203-2013 and supporting G201-2013 and G202-2013 protocols are a good place to start resolving those considerations.

This commitment is therefore required at all levels of the firm, from principals to architectural associates (an AIA-supported term replacing the outdated "intern architect").

Select BIM Software Based on Firm Needs

There is a commonly held assumption that a firm should adopt the same software as everyone else. A particular software application's perceived market share in a few cases may be a legitimate and important consideration, but only if the firm regularly engages in joint ventures or closely teams with firms already using a given software. Most of the time, however, different design disciplines are using different types of software, even by the same software developer. Moreover, architects shouldn't be editing, say, the structural engineer's BIM model, no more than the mechanical engineer should be altering the architect's model files. What's actually relevant is *interoperability*: the capability of design team members and stakeholders to share relevant project information. Having the same software platform doesn't necessarily ensure interoperability due to changes from one release to the next; IFC (Industry Foundation Classes) ensure interoperability. IFC is a neutral, platform-agnostic data format that allows all IFC-compliant authoring software (of which there are many) to import and export. BIM model checking software like Navisworks or Solibri can interpret and compare IFC files from various team members, useful for clash detection and quantity take-offs (see Figure 4.5).

Rarely, an important client may insist on a proprietary file format for project delivery. Often, that's due to a perceived need rather than being an informed requirement. IFC is the appropriate file format for project delivery: all the relevant geometry and data is present and shareable, and the architect (or other design team member) retains authorship of relevant BIM source files (see Figure 4.6). Building owners don't need a natively editable BIM authoring file; they need files that facilities software can use, or that a future design team can reference for expansions and remodels. The US federal government's GSA (Government Services Agency), for example, requires that files be submitted in IFC format, which as stated above most BIM authoring tools support.

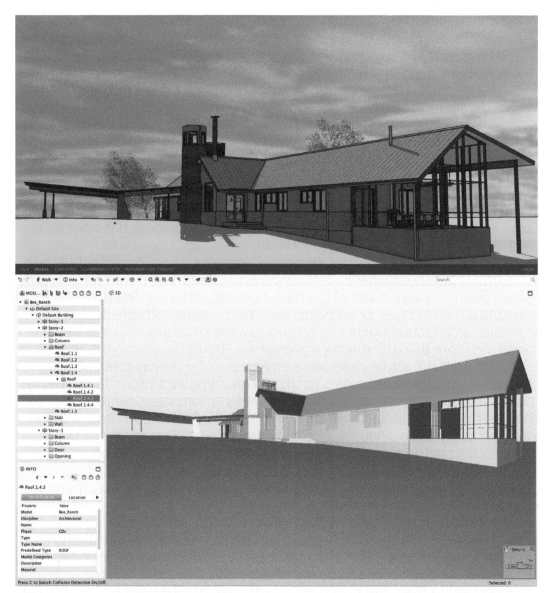

FIGURE 4.5 An IFC file (below) generated in BIM-authoring software (above) and viewed in a model checker.

Consider legitimate reasons for selection of which BIM tools to adopt, since those choices can affect the quality of the design workflow. A firm's principals should become intelligent consumers of technology; if IT technology is outside their skill set, they should delegate that to a competent member of their staff. In considering the firm's particular technological needs, include potential future

FIGURE 4.6 For the Paisano Green Community competition, the Housing Authority of El Paso (HACEP) required BIM submissions, but did not stipulate a particular file format or software choice, leaving it up to the design teams to select their software platforms.

Image courtesy Workshop8, photo credit Jesse Ramirez.

needs. Once a particular platform has been adopted, changing becomes progressively harder over time. Consider:

- **Initial software cost.** This is the most obvious consideration. In the long term, it is also perhaps the least meaningful one.

- **Cost of ownership.** Does the BIM application require an annual subscription, or a perpetual license with an optional added-value subscription plan? Some BIM applications require an annually recurring fee to keep using the software. If the firm changes software, its intellectual property is essentially held hostage.

- **Hardware requirements.** This includes whether the BIM application runs on Macintosh or Windows platforms. Will upgrades be required, or can the application run on some or all of the firm's current hardware?

- **Training costs.** Most firms simply underinvest in training. The expectation is that young architects should have already learned all the software tools they need in school. Moreover, experienced architects are used to recent graduates having to gain most of their practical knowledge of architecture once they are out of school; why shouldn't technological knowledge also be gained on the job?

Investigate similar firms with a project portfolio parallel to the adopting firm, like-minded philosophies of practice, and sympathetic objectives. Ask what BIM applications are in use there, and what they have learned from using them.

- **What are the program's strengths and weaknesses?** What does it do well, and where are there gaps? If the deficiencies aren't critical to the firm's objectives, they might be less of a consideration.

- **What would the other firm have done differently in the process of adopting BIM?** Did they start on one project and ease into BIM, or go all out? Did they spend enough time in training, or learn it ad-hoc? Was their hardware up to the task?

- **What was successful about their implementation of BIM?** Was their first BIM project profitable? Was everyone on the team able to get up to speed? What was it like sharing files with subconsultants? Did BIM positively influence the design outcome?

- **Are the models, drawings, and reports generated by the software communicative to the adopting firm?** If the adopting firm values expressive and communicative drawings with controlled line weights, rendering options ranging from stipples to gradients to variable opacity, then a BIM application that requires the user to struggle to get beautiful drawing output might not be the best choice (see Figure 4.7).

- **Is there a local community of users who can support new users, and whose members are willing to share knowledge?** Are there local user groups? What is the online community of users like? Are online users helpful? How much online content is available?

Start Manageably and Scale Up

Once a firm has acquired BIM technology (including hardware and initial training, formal or otherwise), there are a variety of strategies to help ensure a successful implementation of BIM, some or all of which may be appropriate to a practice, given its particular circumstances.

- **Avoid "shelfware."** Implement BIM and follow through. Investing in the technology and initial training is of no benefit if BIM is not then used. The firm should make a committed effort to producing the next project using BIM.

- **Start with one project.** The above notwithstanding, it may not make sense for a small firm's entire portfolio of current projects to immediately transition to BIM. Select an appropriate new project as a sensible way to expand the practice's technological culture without compromising revenue or the stability of existing project workflows.

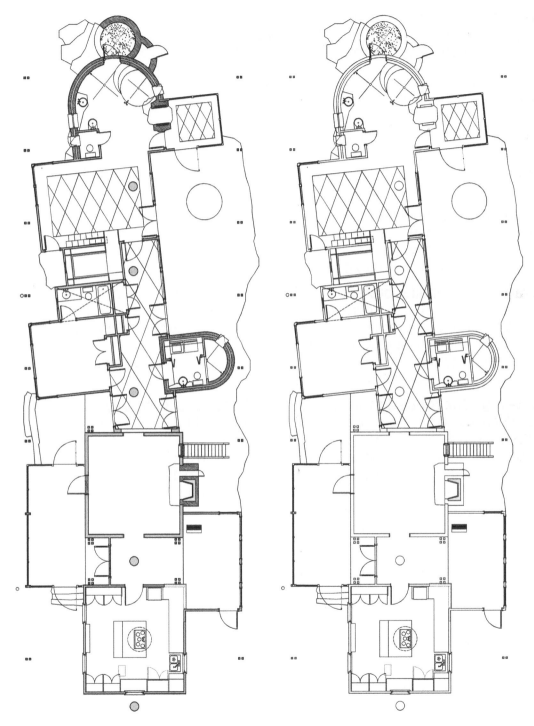

FIGURE 4.7 The same architectural project model in plan view, viewed without concern for line weight or visual communication (bottom), and with expressive line weights and graphic attributes (top).

- **Consider an appropriate and gradual transition.** For the first project, it might also make sense to compartmentalize BIM, initially restricting it to plans, building elevations, and building sections. Alternately, consider limiting BIM to schematic design and design development. Once the design is established, 2D drawing views can be exported and completed in CADD. There will be loss of overall efficiency in this latter approach, as the advantages of deriving a full construction set from the model will not be fully realized. Those losses can be somewhat offset by the benefit of completing the project using familiar CADD processes for the most labor-intensive phase of design. Or the practice might gain enough familiarity in the new process in the first few phases that it may be completed entirely in BIM.

- **Start with a project with limited scope.** If a new project with limited scope is available, the firm may use that as a BIM "shake-out cruise." All the components of the BIM process will be present as a learning test bed. On the other hand, a project with a larger fee may better absorb the initial adoption curve.

- **Start with a familiar project type.** It might be easier to transition to BIM on a common project type where there will be fewer architectural issues outside of BIM to complicate the learning process. In addition, the firm will benefit from having a familiar baseline against which to compare the new process. If your firm does a lot of residential work, a large commercial project might not be the best one to start using BIM.

- **Leverage BIM for design.** It's all too easy to become captivated by BIM's production and documentation efficiency, and lose sight of this book's main thesis. BIM is a powerful design environment with possibilities for leveraging quantitative information to make better design decisions. Starting with your very first BIM projects, look for opportunities to mine your BIM file for quantitative information and use that to inform design. It's fine to begin modestly or prosaically; implementing even coarse cost estimating into your design workflow by developing reports of quantity takeoffs is one example of a basic information task with potentially significant design impacts.

As confidence, skill, and experience grow, the firm can fully transition to BIM. Generally, it is recommended to have only a few transitional projects and to operate fully within a BIM process as quickly as is feasible (see Figure 4.8).

Build on Established Knowledge and Skills

Because BIM evolved from CADD, many CADD skills translate to BIM. The greatest difference between BIM and CADD is a matter of paradigm rather than a question of tasks. The BIM paradigm differs from CADD more significantly than their respective skill requirements. Moreover, a 2D drawing is, in a sense, a model

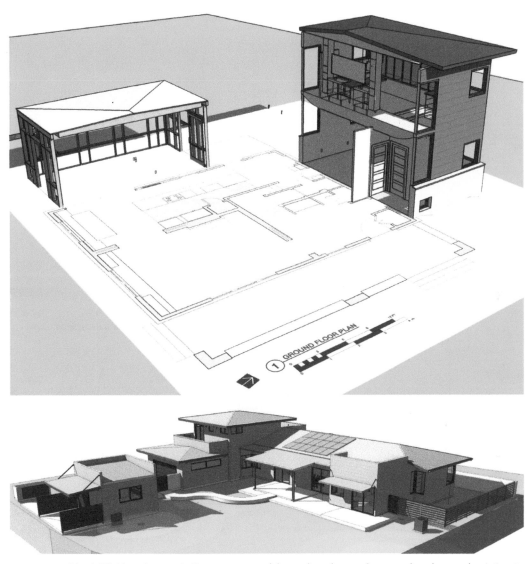

FIGURE 4.8 Start BIM implementation manageably and scale up, from a simpler project (top) to a more complex one (below), for example.

too, albeit a more limited one, and it offers lessons that can be applied to BIM. Namely, a certain level of abstraction is both required and desirable in building information models, just as it is in CADD drawings.

Further, BIM still requires a certain degree of "drafting," if only for annotating views and developing details. Transitioning to BIM does not therefore imply entirely abandoning CADD skills (see Figure 4.9). And as the practice transitions

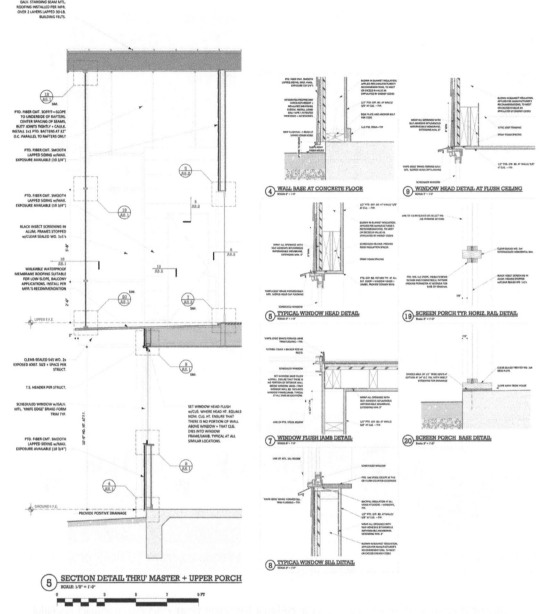

FIGURE 4.9 Certain portions of a drawing set from BIM may be annotated or rendered for increased legibility or detail. BIM model elements like doors and windows are highly simplified, and are not appropriate for head, jamb, and sill details, for example. Here a "pure" BIM section is compared to hybrid "BIM/CADD" details.

fully to a BIM workflow, access to legacy files, such as detail libraries and old projects for reference, will likely be required.

That said, don't deprecate the BIM process. Previous advice to consider transitioning to BIM for early design phases only notwithstanding, avoid using BIM merely as a kind of super sketch modeler, then abandon the building information model in favor of CADD for construction documents. I've known firms, for example, who might develop conceptual models in SketchUp, then use a CADD-capable BIM application like Vectorworks for 2D construction documents (this is particularly egregious as Vectorworks is a fully capable sketch modeler as well as a full BIM-authoring program). Or firms who use SketchUp in schematic design, Revit for design development, and AutoCAD for construction documents. Every time the design transitions from one application to another, two things occur:

1. **Data is lost.** This doesn't mean that gaping holes appear in the model, but rather that inevitably something doesn't translate optimally and needs to be "rebuilt" in the new software. For example, a steel column modeled in SketchUp comes through as an extrusion in ARCHICAD. The geometry may be correct, but it's not a parametric column object. In other words, it doesn't have the "I" in BIM; it's just a mute extrusion.

2. **(Re)design is painful.** I have rarely ever worked on a project when some early-phase design decision, however small, didn't get revisited or changed late in design. Design is simply not in reality a linear process. When a different software application is used for 3D schematic design than for 2D construction documents, the temptation is to make late design revisions only in 2D and avoid modeling them in 3D. After several months of design, there may be significant enough design evolution that the schematic model is hopelessly outdated, so a great deal of revision to it might be required to get it up to date. Thus segregating "design" (3D modeling) from "documentation" (2D construction documents) software effectively creates a software workflow that looks a lot more like the manual drafting and chipboard modeling of Figure 4.1. You might be using BIM tools, but it isn't BIM if you're not also using a BIM workflow (Figure 4.10).

Avoid Backsliding (Get Comfortable with Being Uncomfortable)

I can predict with fair certainty that at some point in your BIM transition, you'll be tempted to go back to a CADD workflow, for a variety of reasons:

◻ **Deadline.** Faced with the pressure of a looming deadline, it might seem like a shortcut to drop BIM and power through with 2D drafting. This is a variation of the training excuse: "We're too busy working to get training." In fact, this is a false economy. You might hit that deadline, but you've just undermined your office BIM culture, and I promise this will bite you later. Hard.

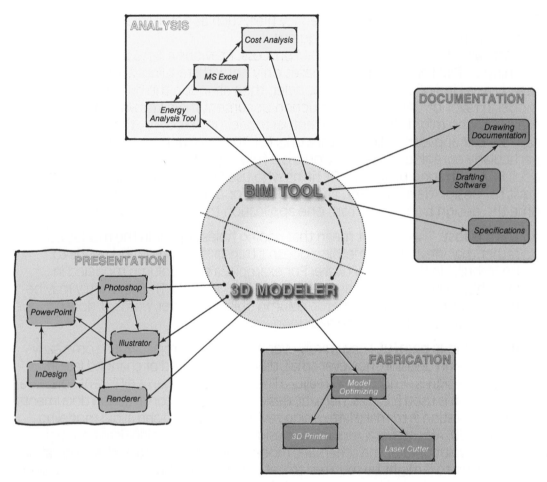

FIGURE 4.10 Impediment to iterative design. If BIM's information capabilities are largely ignored and it is treated as a "super sketch modeler," every data translation to another application is an opportunity for redoing work.

Illustration inspired by presentation graphic by Vectorworks, Inc.

- **Frustration.** I've been using BIM in one form or another for almost 20 years. As a principal in a small firm, I get to use it day in, day out. I wouldn't be truthful if I said there weren't occasional frustrations with technology. Moreover, as I am something of a BIM authority, colleagues and professional associates frequently approach me for technical support (the other day I got a texted plea for help during an intermission of a screening of *Gone with the Wind*, and I've even given tech support while on a run). I may not have seen it all, but I've seen quite a lot. The vast majority of the time, frustration is due to incomplete understanding or misunderstanding of the software. In other words, lack of training or inadequate training. Sometimes it's due to unrealistic expectations of what software can do. (Frankly, unrealistic expectations arise from ignorance of what the software can or can't do—in other words, it's a function of lack of training.) Occasionally, there's a bug in the software. Do your community a favor: if you think you found a bug, file it with the software developer.

□ **Resistance.** In spite of what's been said in "Making a Firm Commitment" above, you may have staff who resist BIM. You have a few options, most of which are bad. Reassign them to tasks that don't touch or lightly BIM (specification writing, construction administration, client contact, selections). For most firms, that's probably unrealistic. Or you can persuade them to get on the BIM train. The caution here is that they need a wholehearted transformation in their attitude towards BIM. Force won't, in the long run, work. The last option is to let them go. See "Hiring for A(p)ttitude" below.

□ **Skill loss.** Sometimes staff with key BIM skills leave the firm. Subsequently, it may be tempting to abandon or sideline your BIM workflow. The lesson here is that BIM requires a cultural shift in your entire firm (make a firm commitment!). Train everyone. Don't allow anyone to become the indispensable gatekeeper, not by undermining your BIM star, but by building your entire team to be BIM players (see Figure 4.11).

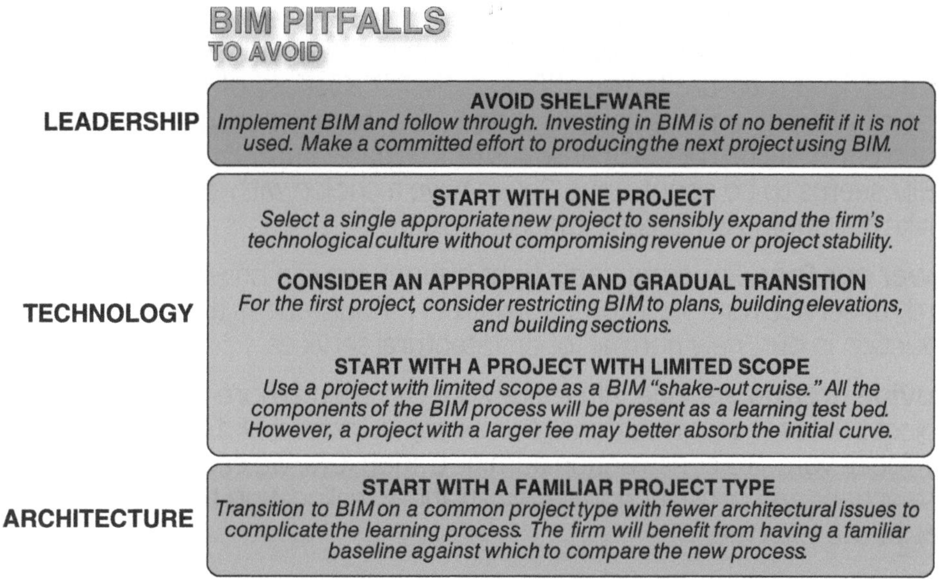

BIM PITFALLS
TO AVOID

LEADERSHIP	**AVOID SHELFWARE** Implement BIM and follow through. Investing in BIM is of no benefit if it is not used. Make a committed effort to producing the next project using BIM.
TECHNOLOGY	**START WITH ONE PROJECT** Select a single appropriate new project to sensibly expand the firm's technological culture without compromising revenue or project stability. **CONSIDER AN APPROPRIATE AND GRADUAL TRANSITION** For the first project, consider restricting BIM to plans, building elevations, and building sections. **START WITH A PROJECT WITH LIMITED SCOPE** Use a project with limited scope as a BIM "shake-out cruise." All the components of the BIM process will be present as a learning test bed. However, a project with a larger fee may better absorb the initial curve.
ARCHITECTURE	**START WITH A FAMILIAR PROJECT TYPE** Transition to BIM on a common project type with fewer architectural issues to complicate the learning process. The firm will benefit from having a familiar baseline against which to compare the new process.

FIGURE 4.11 Pitfalls to avoid, strategies to take in adopting a sustainable BIM workflow.

A few years ago, I was commissioned to design a very modest kitchen remodel and addition—a small bedroom and bathroom on the ground floor, and a master bathroom above—for a historic home in Austin, near the University of Texas. Partly out of a misplaced nostalgia for the CADD old days, I decided to do the project entirely in 2D. By the time the project was in design development, I was miserable. Every little change in plan had to be manually traced through all the sheets of my little drawing set, a perfectly normal process with CADD. BIM-steeped as I was by then, I found this once-normal process irritating. Mid-design, I stopped, took the time to model the existing house and the addition, and got back on the BIM track. The rest of design development and CDs went smoothly from that point forward. I became freer to design millwork and built-ins, and incorporated perspectives of a bench, kitchen island, and study overlook in the CDs. Come permitting, the Plan Review department insisted that I demonstrate that less than half the portion of the attic that was over five feet (1.5 m) tall was also under seven feet (2.1 m) tall. Given the complexity of the roof geometry (a nearly pyramidal hipped roof with a slightly different dormer in each cardinal direction), I was able to section the BIM model and quickly provided the required documentation (Figure 4.12). BIM was easier, faster, and more pleasurable to work in, and saved me from a permitting headache.

It's perfectly natural to tend to revert to the familiar. Don't backslide. The way up is through.

Adjust Contracts to Align with Your BIM Processes

In our firm, empirically we've found that we can produce the equivalent design and documentation work in about 70% of the time with BIM than with CADD. That's a difficult measure to quantify exactly, for a variety of reasons: every project is different, and we haven't used CADD for other than details in several years, so our baseline for comparison is out of date. But 30% greater efficiency with BIM seems to be about right. So we have a choice with every project, which we make depending on circumstances. We can:

□ **Lower our fees.** For clients on a tight budget, we can provide a "CADD standard" of service for a very competitive fee. I should stress that this represents a reduction in our "new normal" of architectural services.

□ **Provide greater service.** Alternately, we can spend more time in architectural project phases than is traditional. For example, instead of a perfunctory 15% of our fee devoted to construction administration (CA), we can get highly involved in selections and construction administration, reallocating the CA fee to about 30% of the total fee.

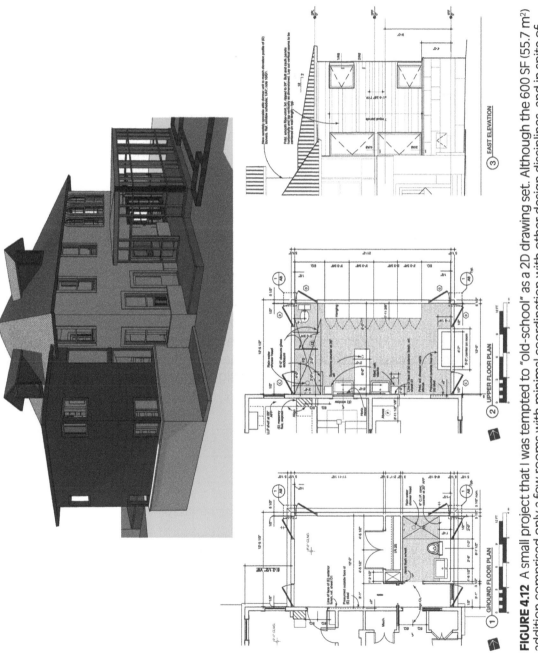

FIGURE 4.12 A small project that I was tempted to "old-school" as a 2D drawing set. Although the 600 SF (55.7 m²) addition comprised only a few rooms with minimal coordination with other design disciplines, and in spite of the fact that it became a BIM project mid-stream, it was still more efficient and effective to develop this as a BIM project.

111

❑ **Provide better service.** Or, we can design with greater depth in any given phase. For example, our schematic design deliverables may be greater than is customary, or our design development drawings may include deliverables that we might otherwise included in construction documents. Naturally, we inherently capitalize on design opportunities with BIM whenever we can, from sustainable design to improved visualization.

In practice, the distinctions between the above three approaches get blurry. With BIM, we can keep our fees a little lower than we otherwise would set them in order to be more competitive, *and* expand both the quantity *and* quality of service that we provide. The point is to keep track of how you and your staff actually spend your time, and adjust your fees and scope of services accordingly (Figure 4.13).

Training and Workflow

As should be evident throughout this book, at its best BIM demands new ways of designing, a paradigm shift in the design process that is as much cognitive as it is procedural. There are three major areas in which BIM differs radically and paradigmatically from most traditional design processes: real-time derivation of 2D drawings from digital models; information-rich 3D objects supported by a queryable database, and interoperability. *Workflow* is a term that describes certain aspects of that paradigm shift. *Training*, on the other hand, is merely the learning of specific tasks. Both are required for successful BIM implementation. Performing BIM tasks without a shift in design processes is like taking a

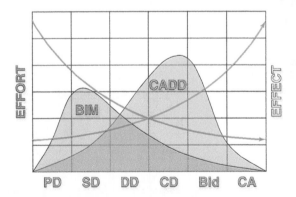

FIGURE 4.13 The MacLeamy curve, credited to Patrick MacLeamy of HOK, is one of many representations of the inherent "left shift" of design processes that require additional work earlier in the design process. MacLeamy's original diagram was intended to represent the work distribution associated with IPD (integrated project delivery), but it is equally applicable to non-IPD BIM.

road trip without a map; attempting to adopt a new workflow without a strong foundation in appropriate tasks is like taking a road trip without a car.

Architects, long trained to mentally project and imagine three-dimensional space on the basis of reading and creating two-dimensional abstract projections, must embrace a three-dimensional workflow. We've discussed some of that inertia and speculated as to possible causes. Nevertheless it's essential; moreover, it's not as alien to design methodologies as one might think. Medieval architects (master masons and carpenters) built scale models of cathedrals, a tradition that was parameterized by the artistically mystical and brilliant Antoni Gaudí (see Figure 4.14). Certainly the Beaux Arts tradition was no stranger to plaster maquettes.

3D modeling alone, as has been emphasized, does not a BIM workflow make. Throughout this book and particularly in the next two chapters we look at case

FIGURE 4.14 One of Antoni Gaudí's hanging weight models in the Museo de la Sagrada Familia. The Catalan architect famously used weights suspended from lengths of chains to create catenary curves that responded to gravity loads. Gaudí had the insight that the shape of the loaded catenary would be horizontally symmetrical to a loaded arch; by measuring the loaded chains and flipping the derived form upside-down, complex catenary arches and vaults could be built that would withstand gravity load. In a real sense, this design by simulation was an analog precursor to parametric modeling and BIM.

Image ©2009 Canaan / Wikimedia Commons, licensed under the Creative Commons Attribution-Share Alike 4.0 International.

studies underscoring the critical importance of the "I" in BIM. Data plays a role in BIM design processes for form-based zoning compliance, site analysis, passive energy design (from shading and thermal envelope performance to passive cooling and heating), structural analysis, coordination between trades and divisions, cost analysis and value engineering, and fabrication, to name but a few applications.

Finally, a data-rich building model has the fertile potential for interoperability and integration, whereby disparate design disciplines contribute to a federated model comprising architectural, structural, civil, MEP (mechanical, electrical, and plumbing), and lighting systems (Figure 4.15). Such a combined models require transformative levels of communication between team members, not merely at the technological level (new and evolving file formats like IFC for interoperability), but particularly at the social level. Architecture and engineering becomes much more of a collaborative team effort.

FIGURE 4.15 A federated BIM model integrating architectural, structural, and MEP (mechanical, electrical, and plumbing) systems. Here, individual models have been developed in their respective BIM authoring platforms, then integrated via the IFC (Industry Foundation Classes) format and viewed, checked, and surveyed via a BIM model checker like Solibri or Navisworks.

Image courtesy of Vectorworks, Inc.

Investing in training. Without a solid foundation in the at-times prosaic tasks required to fully capitalize on the BIM authoring software of choice, understanding the BIM paradigm shift is merely academic. Training is absolutely critical, particularly given the inherent complexities of data-rich building models. Many small firms especially skimp on training, and as a result are far less productive than they could be, missing opportunities to be fully enabled in their BIM use for both design and production. In the not-so-long run, training pays for itself, with dividends. Without training, powerful features that may be present in software the firm already owns and deploys might be overlooked. I've been approached countless times by fellow architects impressed with some "new" feature of the software, only to tell them it was introduced several years before—they just never became aware of it.

Yet it should be acknowledged that training does represent a nontrivial investment. Formal classroom training or individual tutoring itself costs money, and staff must be compensated for their time attending; if the training is not available locally, travel expenses may be incurred. Moreover, time spent training is time away from billable work, so there are meaningful opportunity costs. For those firms that do not have the financial capacity to send staff to attend dedicated training courses, there are fortunately numerous free (albeit scattered) training resources for many BIM software applications (see Figure 4.16). Some useful cost-effective training strategies include:

- **Free web resources.** Search the software developer's website for free training resources, as well as training guides and YouTube channels promulgated by dedicated users with useful video tips and tutorials. The upside is that you will doubtless find countless videos and short tutorials. The downside is that these resources tend not to be organized or curated, and you may have to spend a fair amount of time finding appropriate materials. The problem with informal training is that it can be rather scattershot and rely on happenstance. Self-training with online videos is not the same as attending a training course, whether that course is held in a classroom, on site, or online. This kind of self-training can be a bit like reading a book one random page at a time; you might eventually read and understand all the words in the book, but you'll have a confused sense of the narrative and be missing a lot of context.

- **Designated driver.** Assign those firm members with the most technological inclination and interest to collect and organize training material and build a training library. This could be a collection of Internet links logically organized, but it will have to be periodically updated and old resources verified.

- **Buy a book, and use it.** Any worthwhile BIM authoring platform will have an online users manual that explains every individual tool and command for using

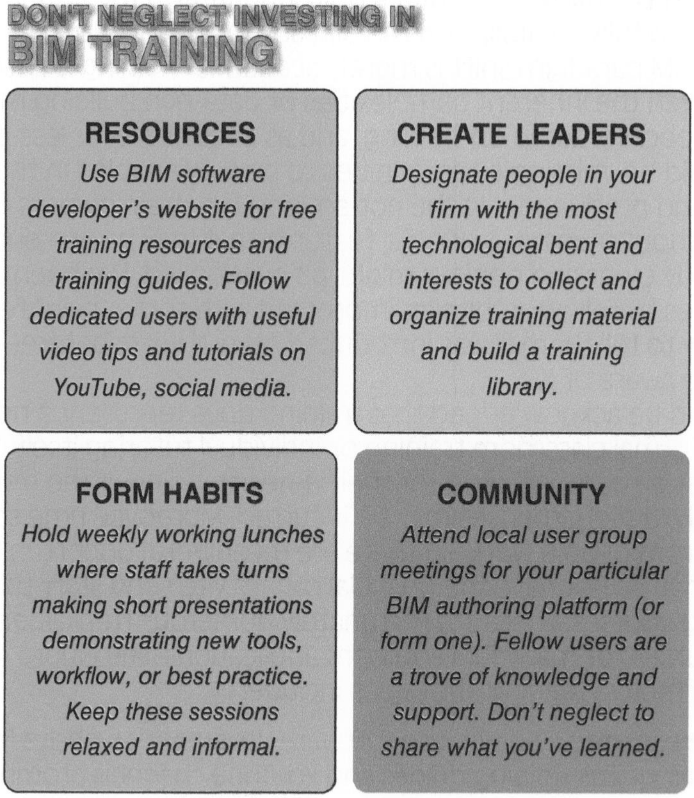

DON'T NEGLECT INVESTING IN
BIM TRAINING

RESOURCES
Use BIM software developer's website for free training resources and training guides. Follow dedicated users with useful video tips and tutorials on YouTube, social media.

CREATE LEADERS
Designate people in your firm with the most technological bent and interests to collect and organize training material and build a training library.

FORM HABITS
Hold weekly working lunches where staff takes turns making short presentations demonstrating new tools, workflow, or best practice. Keep these sessions relaxed and informal.

COMMUNITY
Attend local user group meetings for your particular BIM authoring platform (or form one). Fellow users are a trove of knowledge and support. Don't neglect to share what you've learned.

FIGURE 4.16 Numerous training opportunities are available in addition to established hands-on classroom training, which is nevertheless quite effective.

the software. But users manuals can be a bit like the introduction to Prokofiev's *Peter and the Wolf*: each musical instrument represents a single character. It isn't until all the musicians play together that one understands "orchestra." Likewise, most user manuals aren't designed to provide an overarching context of how the various BIM tools work together. For that, find a training manual, designed around an intentional curriculum so as to teach how the tools work together. Video manuals have become popular, often accompanied by sample files. It might be a good idea to watch a video manual on a tablet or device, while following along using your BIM software on a computer. Other users may learn better with old-school, wire-bound book (easy to lay flat). Either way, training books are a cost-effective way to learn BIM software in a logical, comprehensive, structured format.

- **Sponsor a weekly office working lunch** where staff is encouraged to take turns making short presentations demonstrating a new tool, workflow, or best practice. Keep these learning sessions relaxed and informal, and short (an hour or so at most).

- **Attend user group meetings** for your particular BIM authoring platform (or form one if there isn't already one). Other users are a trove of free knowledge and support. Don't neglect to share what your firm has learned. Once your firm has developed a strong skill base, stick around and pass on your knowledge.

- **Sign up for online classes.** Also growing in popularity, online courses are typically offered through professional training venues, whether offered by the BIM software developer, specialized sites like ArchonCad.com or general ones like Lynda.com, or some universities. While the personal attention one gets in a physical classroom can be very helpful, online training can be far less expensive, and more flexible.

Bear in mind that training tends to imply task-oriented learning and might not fully address the design process implications of BIM. In addition to training, firms that successfully transition to BIM might also reorganize their design processes, and even how they go about project delivery.

Impact of Training. The smaller the firm, the greater the number of roles each individual generally assumes, and the more vital the role each individual plays. For a firm with a handful of staff, one missing person represents a significant loss of productivity and billing. One of the greatest BIM challenges that small firms face therefore is the temporary reduction in output as staff undergo training, and the time it takes for newly trained staff to "get up to speed." Eventually a well-implemented BIM workflow should yield significant efficiency and productivity gains and even allow the firm to offer new services. But in the short term, it might seem that productivity decreases. On the other hand, the larger the firm, the greater its "technological inertia." Changing a handful of people's software habits can be far easier than changing those of scores of people.

However, in most cases BIM requires that users have a greater understanding of building components and their relationship to the project. Experienced designers must therefore closely mentor junior architects, and workflows that rely on blindly drafting details will need to be reevaluated. On the other hand, a smaller team with greater architectural expertise can leverage that very effectively with BIM.

Moreover, when work is abundant it is extremely difficult to set it aside and make time for training, much less implement the radically new workflows that

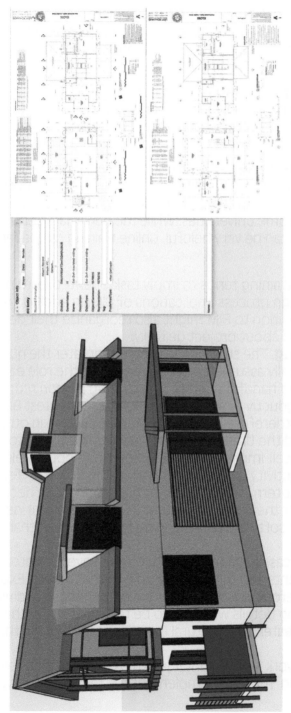

FIGURE 4.17 When sharing BIM models, it's a good practice to include PDFs at minimum (top right) if not 2D vector drawings like DWG files (bottom right), along with the IFC model (left).

transitioning from BIM to CADD represents. When the pendulum swings the other way and work tapers off, it becomes difficult to budget for training. Add to this the reluctance some might have to learn what can be perceived as yet another software application, and it is clear why many firms make training a low priority. Yet training is both an essential and recurring requirement; firms ignore or defer it at their peril.

Sharing. An important characteristic of a BIM workflow is its transformation of data sharing (drawings and models) with others. Here are a few points to consider:

- **Incorporate LOD in your BIM culture.** See Brian Skripac's Level of Development article in Chapter 2.

- **Manage BIM.** It's important to agree on who is responsible for what aspect of the model(s), within your firm and between subconsultants, and a schedule for sharing models, and to establish clash detection milestones. Again, the above-mentioned AIA exhibit and protocols can be very useful. Even if you don't use these documents as part of your contracts, use them as a tool to help ferret out potential issues and map out a BIM management strategy.

- **Test.** Before you begin a project, exchange sample files with subconsultants. You'll probably use IFC files to exchange BIM models with others on the design team outside your office. When you send IFC files, send PDFs and DWGs with them for corroboration and verification (Figure 4.17).

Hire for A(p)ttitude

There is an assumption held by both staff and employers that it's critical for staff to have BIM skills in order to be employable. While it's certainly true that architectural staff must be able to acquire and expand BIM-related skills, hiring someone based on a list of task-based skills is probably a mistake. All BIM-authoring software operates under the same principles, regardless of the nuances of their varied implementation of this principles and their individuated feature sets. I have found that a positive attitude, intellectual curiosity, and open-mindedness are greater predictors of successful co-workers than a high aptitude with a specific software application. New tools can far more easily be learned than negative attitudes discarded.

Chapter 5

Case Studies in Form Making

This chapter unpacks a series of project case studies—some granular, others more general—that help illustrate and underscore the role of investigation in reconciling conflicting design constraints, as well as pointing to the role of BIM design processes in formulating design solutions. Much of the emphasis is on the use of BIM-authoring software as a modeling and to a certain extent simulation environment.

Introduction

In architecture, there is commonly a deep regard for the geometry or physical form of a building or other design element, what is often referred to in the parlance as a "formal" concern (not "formal" in the sense of "according to convention"). For many, if not most, designers—and I admit to being in this group—there is a fundamental drive to create satisfying forms. Of course, what constitutes "satisfying" may be a function of personal taste, cultural expectations, professional norms, and even what is simply fashionable. Given too much free reign, formal concerns swamp the design and may lead to self-indulgent solutions that prioritize pure form over solving for design constraints such as program, client expectations, the application of appropriate building technologies, cost, building performance, durability, and so on. In other words, the design risks overwhelming Vitruvius's *firmitas* and *utilitas* with a disproportionate concern for a highly personal sense of *venustas*.

There is design as a noun, and there is design as a verb. To design is to problem solve, and beyond merely solving for one variable. A simple design problem has by definition one or more obvious solutions. In the simple case, "design" is the selection of a solution based on personal preferences or inclinations. For design to be a process worthy of thoughtful consideration, it must address complex or inobvious problems. In one view, to design is to reconcile the irreconcilable. When a design problem has only one constraint, or when all constraints are in agreement with one another, the design solution is self-evident and contained within the constraints themselves. A single constraint is thus just a prescription. When multiple constraints compete with one another, contradict one another, clash with one another, then there arises an opportunity for something new. Without contradiction, there can be no narrative. Without conflicting constraints, there is no design. Without adversity, there can be no triumph.

Out of the nature of design arise three consequences. First, it is incumbent on the designer to understand the particular individual constraints of a given design problem thoroughly and intimately. Second, the designer must uncover those areas where constraints conflict, for it is in the mechanisms of contradictory constraints that the opportunities for overcoming them manifest. (As the reader might suspect, information-rich digital modeling is an eloquent vehicle for the investigation demanded by design.)

Third, in the resolution of those constraints there emerges an opportunity for the unexpected. As a designer, I know that I am on to something when an unexpected design solution surfaces, of which I had no inkling when I began to work. There are many instances when those solutions seem to come from somewhere else. Perhaps they seem to do so because they were subconsciously with me all along. Yet I suspect that surprising solutions arise out of an immersion in understanding the design problem's constraints, rather than from prefabricated formal notions. In other words, the contradictions of the problem themselves suggest successful solutions, rather than solutions being imposed on the problem.

The Case Studies

Case Study: Stating the Problem

In many jurisdictions in the United States, municipalities have responded to the ever-increasing size of detached single-family residences with the formulation of form-based codes intended to reign in the bloat of the McMansion. These ordinances vary in their scope and implementation, but have in common that they seek a formulaic and legalistic solution to an architectural problem. As each seemingly isolated issue comes to a city council's attention, a disconnected hodgepodge of at times contradictory ordinances grows up over time: compatibility standards for adjacent disparate zonings, building setbacks, solar rights, tree protection, impervious cover limitations, floor-area-ratio restrictions, and of course anti-McMansionization.

And as wellmeaning as these zoning codes may be, their intent of preserving neighborhood character and compatible scale at times creates unintended consequences. Arguably, as lots in older and desirable central city neighborhoods become less developable due to the increasing zoning restrictions placed upon them, they become more valuable, and affordable housing suffers accordingly. Moreover, sprawl is encouraged, as potential homebuilders and -buyers move to the suburbs and exurbs seeking relief from land use restrictions.

Fortunately for design professionals, in some US cities it has become nearly impossible to build a home in such neighborhoods without an architect, as the accretion of individual ordinances creates a bewildering array of restrictions that the average layman cannot unravel without considerable effort. But pity the poor architect, who must determine the buildable volume of a project as early in the design process as possible, or risk designing an unpermittable project. BIM to the rescue!

Consider as a case in point Subchapter F of the Land Development Code for Austin, Texas, that went into effect in 2006 and was amended slightly in 2008. This so-called McMansion ordinance affects one- and two-family dwellings within a broad central 67-square-mile (174 km²) area loosely conforming to Austin's early 1970s-era boundaries. Within this area:

- **Floor-area-ratio (FAR) is limited to 0.4.** Generally, a residential project's developed square footage cannot exceed 40% of the lot's projected (plan) area. There are exemptions for spaces under five feet tall, and (with limitations) for porches, garages, carports, basements at least 50% underground, and attics not exceeding seven feet (2.1 m) in height over 50% of their area at least five feet (1.5 m) tall.

- **Form-based tent.** With exceptions for gables, shed roofs, and incidental projections, no portion of the building may extend beyond an imaginary "tent." The boundary of this volume is determined by dividing the lot into 40 foot (12.2 m) sections, beginning with the street-most portion of the house, and continuing back from the street until the rear of the lot is reached. The sides of this "tent" are vertical and 15 feet (4.6 m) tall, then slope at a 45° angle away from the side lot line. The starting elevation of the vertical portion is taken from the highest of four points, where the two boundaries of the 40 foot zone parallel to the street meet the two side lot lines. The rear of the tent similarly slopes up away from the rear lot line; the street face of the tent is gabled (vertical). It should be evident that this description presupposes a rectangular lot; if the site is irregular (say, triangular), it may be unclear which is the rear lot line.

- **Overall height.** The maximum overall height of a home is 32 feet (9.8 m), measured from the average of the highest and lowest adjacent natural grades, to the midpoint of the roof if gabled or a shed, or to the top of the parapet if a flat roof.

The above is a somewhat simplified explanation in the interest of brevity, but it may underscore the opportunities for accurately determining design boundaries with data-rich models.

▫ The **automation of FAR calculations**, updated in real time as the design evolves, is a mundane but essential design task for which BIM is well suited. Various occupancies (conditioned space, porches, garages, carports, and so forth) can populate a total floor area schedule or tool, and be compared to the lot area; the designer can verify total FAR at any time in the design process.

▫ It should be evident from Figure 5.1 that while the "tent" might be readily drawn as a 2D construction given a fairly flat and regularly shaped lot, **an irregular boundary and uneven topography almost requires 3D modeling**. A digital site model with elevation-aware "stake" points is invaluable in determining the starting elevation of the tent zones, as well as average adjacent grade. The tent itself can be easily modeled by repurposing BIM authoring software's roof tool, as a series of 40 foot long virtual open-end gables with a structural depth at or approaching 0.

Case Study: Double Cantilever

Even in speculative, single-family detached infill projects, there are opportunities for structural expressiveness. In the case of Cedar Fever, a modest, 1,750 sf (163 m²) three-bedroom house, a restricted program, building setbacks, and

FIGURE 5.1 In some cases, an intelligent (i.e., data-rich) digital model is required even at preliminary design stages to establish the constraints of form-based codes. Here, an actual central-city site in Austin, Texas, has both atypical metes and bounds and significant topography. The McMansion "tent" boundary (in red) could not have been feasibly determined without digital modeling.

adjacent heritage trees with protected root zones limit the buildable footprint. Rather than design a separate, dedicated covered parking structure, the project's carport is conceived as a northern extension of the front porch roof, while the horizontal plane of the roof continues uninterrupted to shelter the south-eastern screened porch (Figure 5.2). Ideally, the "carport" can fulfill its stated function of sheltering an automobile, or alternately serve as a covered outdoor space for gatherings or leisure. It is thus both a programmatic as well as a structural extension of the front porch.

Yet the carport function combined with building setbacks imposes certain structural limitations. By local code, roofs are allowed to extend up to two feet (0.6 m) into the five foot (1.5 m) side setback. A column at the northeast corner of the carport would be structurally welcome, but would make the relatively modest covered area difficult to negotiate while parking an automobile and almost plead for an accident. Moreover, the architectural gesture of a somewhat flat porch roof serves as foil to the high pitch of the main mass of the house; hence the strong, horizontal line of the porch roof. A low-pitched hip porch

FIGURE 5.2 This modest single-family detached home in central east Austin, Texas employs a low-pitched hipped roof with asymmetrical roof slopes to cover a screened porch, entry porch, and carport.

roof potentially resolves these disparate architectural, programmatic, and structural agendas.

The low pitch of the roof supported the desired architectural gesture, and each face of the three-sided hipped structure was given a unique pitch such that both the fascia and intersection of the roof with the house's exterior walls are level. The roof was modeled from an intelligent BIM object, incorporating parametric information such as plate height, roof face pitches, eave profile and overhang, and appearance.

The volume of the BIM roof object established the boundary within which a structural solution for the northeast cantilever of the roof could be resolved. The model was shared with the project's structural engineer, Michelle Weinfeld, who engineered a double cantilever and sized the beams.

The preliminary structural model was passed back to the author, who refined the framing of the roof using parametric framing objects, subject to the engineer's approval. The final framing model was compared to the architectural roof to ensure it was enclosed within the roof boundaries (Figure 5.3).

Case Study: Hope House

Hope House of Austin (www.hopehouseaustin.org) is a nonprofit assisted living organization and facility whose mission is to provide a "supportive, permanent home where residents with profound mental and physical challenges are happy and free to realize their potential." Its original purpose to care for children with extreme needs has been extended over the years as residents have matured into adulthood, and its housing requirements have outstripped its central facility. As a result, the organization has in more recent times adopted a strategy of creating satellite homes within the community of Liberty Hill 30 miles from Austin, Texas, where adult residents can live and receive 24-hour care. Lévy Kohlhaas Architects was approached by Hope House to design a duplex for eight residents, four bedrooms per unit (Figure 5.4).

Both client and architect recognized that as challenging as it would be to pay for a new residence, meeting maintenance costs would be an ongoing struggle. They therefore resolved that the home should be durable and with as small an energy footprint as practical given a restricted construction budget, adopting these design strategies:

- **Efficient use of space.** In an effort to control construction scope and therefore cost, a key design objective was for the duplex to be as small as possible while still meeting resident and staff needs. Moreover, a central tenet of Hope House's operational philosophy is to engage residents in outdoor activities as much as possible. Minimizing built space therefore had the mission-supporting benefit of encouraging outdoor activities.

FIGURE 5.3 The resulting structural model of the roof, designed in close collaboration with the structural engineer (also a BIM user), is visually compared with the architectural model in order to check that the structure lies within the architectural boundaries of roof decking and soffit.

□ **Maximize passive thermal controls.** The site is a generous small-town lot of a third of an acre (14,390 sf or 1,337 m²), so there was great flexibility in siting the 2,421 sf (225 m²) building. The final design has an aspect ratio emphasizing a long east-west axis for maximum northern and southern exposure. North light is fairly benign for summer heat gain, and southern light is relatively easy to control with appropriate overhangs. East and west orientations are minimized, limiting exposure to low, intense morning and afternoon summer solar insolation (Figure 5.5).

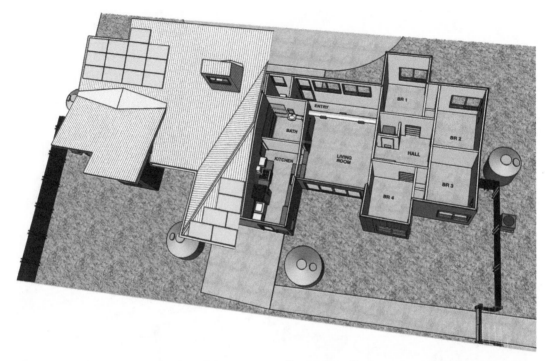

FIGURE 5.4 Cutaway perspective of Hope House, illustrating the long aspect ratio, symmetry of plan, and room arrangement.

- **Deploy scalable active sustainability features.** It was not clear at the onset of design whether certain sustainable systems such as a photovoltaic array or rainwater harvesting system would be within the budget, and whether donors might come forth to help provide them. The project was designed with a scalable approach to such systems. Roof planes were pitched to optimize summer solar collection and the building prewired for a PV system, whether installed during construction or retrofitted. A metal roof and appropriate guttering were specified to facilitate rainwater harvesting, even if collection cisterns were to be added later (Figure 5.6).

- **Indoor-outdoor connection.** Windows in all the bedrooms were maximized within the constraints of the building envelope's total thermal performance, in order to provide visual connection to the outside, plentiful but controlled daylighting, and egress. Large glass sliding doors detailed with a minimal threshold provide a nearly six-foot-wide (1.83 m) opening from each unit to a shared yard, for ease of transfer to the outdoors.

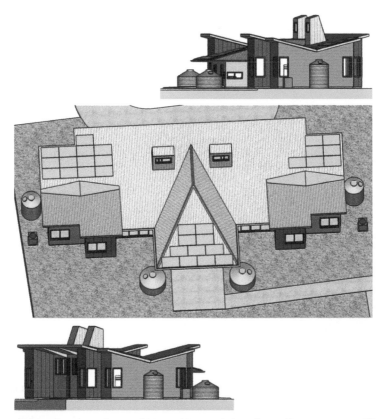

FIGURE 5.5 Parallel projection views of Hope House taken from three sun positions on September 20, near the autumnal equinox. At this time of year the sun path is lower than at midsummer, thus defeating roof overhangs for more of the day than at the summer solstice, but daytime temperatures are still high. With this project's orientation, at sunrise (upper right) and sunset (lower left) there is minimal solar exposure (insolation); at noon (middle) the roof surfaces shield the wall envelope from the majority of solar gain. The metal roof is reflective, and the roof structure is more heavily insulated than the walls.

Resolving conflicting constraints: thermal chimney and PV. In hot, humid climates like that of Central Texas, ventilation is the most effective passive cooling strategy, as it displaces the human psychrometric comfort zone into a warmer, more humid area of the chart (Figure 5.7). For those days when there is no wind-driven airflow, Hope House employs twin thermal chimneys to naturally ventilate each unit, exploiting the stack effect, warm air's natural buoyancy. This passive cooling technique is centuries old: warm air rises, is evacuated from a high aperture, and entrains lower, cooler air to move throughout the space.

RAINWATER HARVESTING

DESIGN DATA

AVAILABLE ROOF FOOTPRINT	3,097 FT2
HARVEST CAPABILITY	51,336 GAL

OCCUPANCY (OFF-GRID ONLY)

OCCUPANTS	0
DAILY CONSUMPTION	40 GAL
DROUGHT	100
OCCUPANT CONSUMPTION	0 GAL

IRRIGATION

GARDEN	1,350 FT2
REQUIREMENTS	1 IN
RAINFALL AREA COEFFICIENT	0.623
LENGTH OF SUMMER	17.5 WKS
REQUIRED WATER	14,726 GAL
SUMMER RAINFALL (JUNE-SEPT)	3.7 IN
NATURAL RAINFALL RECEIVED	3,116 GAL
DEFICIT	11,610 GAL
SUMMER ROOF HARVEST	5,963 GAL
IRRIGATION REQUIREMENT	5,646 GAL

STORAGE REQUIRED

	5,646 GAL
VOLUME	755 FT3
CORGAL 0602-WT-FS-25	1,500 GAL
CORGAL 0801-WT-FS-25	1,300 GAL
INSTALLED CAPACITY	5,600 GAL

RAINFALL DATA

J	1.71 IN
F	2.17 IN
M	1.87 IN
A	2.56 IN
M	4.78 IN
J	3.72 IN
J	2.04 IN
A	2.05 IN
S	3.3 IN
O	3.43 IN
N	2.37 IN
D	1.88 IN
ANNUAL RAINFALL	**31.88 IN**
ANNUAL EVAPORATION	90 IN
ANNUAL EVAPORATION	7.5 FT
GAL./INCH RAIN/ROOF FT2	0.52
GALLONS PER FT3	7.48

FIGURE 5.6 Hope House is on the municipal water system, so rainwater harvesting for potable water is not permissible due to concerns for potential cross-contamination of the public water system. However, water harvesting for irrigating the site's extensive grounds is permitted, and the roof design allows for incremental scaling of water storage as needed.

The ASHRAE *Handbook of Fundamentals* has for decades included a formula to estimate the rate of air flow from the stack effect based on several variables, many of which can be harvested from a BIM: relative areas of and vertical distance between lower and upper apertures, and inlet and outlet temperatures. In the worksheet built into the BIM file (Figure 5.8), all but the temperature values are automatically supplied by the model itself; the later are user-provided estimates.

The taller the thermal chimney, the greater the air flow it can produce, but the longer the shadow it casts—literally—on the photovoltaic array. While PV controls have improved in recent years to help mitigate shading losses, partial shading of an array is still undesirable and disproportionately affects its overall

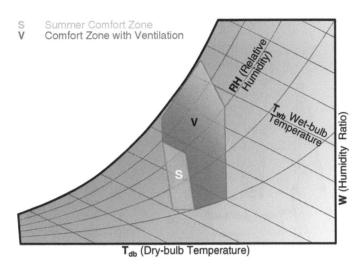

S   Summer Comfort Zone
V   Comfort Zone with Ventilation

FIGURE 5.7 Providing natural ventilation does not necessarily significantly cool a space, but it does work with biological cooling mechanisms to alter the human perception of comfort, effectively relocating the "comfort zone" on the psychrometric chart such that occupants feel more comfortable in warmer, more humid conditions.

performance. To resolve this conflict, a first-order quantitative analysis was undertaken, using the information from the virtual building:

▫ A preliminary energy analysis of internal and external energy loads— using Vectorworks Architect's Energos module and the US Department of Energy's National Renewal Energy Laboratory's PV Watts web tool (pvwatts .nrel.gov)—suggested that an 11 kW PV array should achieve net-zero performance. To be clear, net-zero was not a part of the project brief, nor was an 11 kW array expected to be installed initially. However, for the sake of future improvements to the project, a plausible path to net-zero should not be excluded. If possible, the irony of the passive cooling thermal chimney reducing the effectiveness of the PV array should be avoided.

▫ The number of modules required to achieve 11 kW of generation was esti- mated using the performance and dimensional data of a commonly available photovoltaic module, and the National Renewable Energy Laboratory's online PVWatts tool (pvwatts.nrel.gov). The array modules were then included in the model.

▫ The air movement generated by the thermal chimneys was estimated using the basic hand-coded ASHRAE stack effect calculator in the BIM file. As the design was refined, the calculations were updated in real time to ascertain performance loss, if any, from later thermal chimney design iterations.

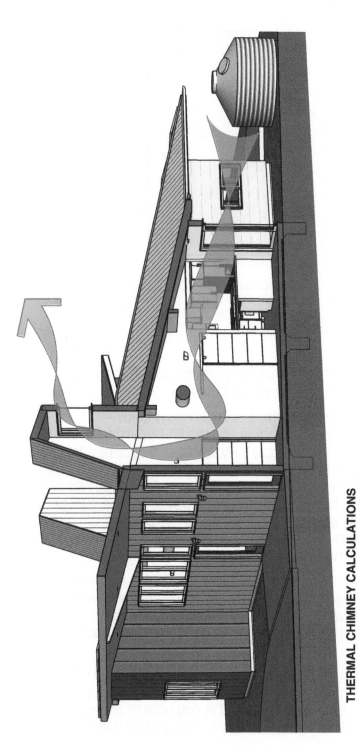

THERMAL CHIMNEY CALCULATIONS

Cd	T in °F	T out °F	A, LOWER SQ FT	A, UPPER SQ FT	A RATIO	K	g FT/S·S	Z, BASE FT	Z, TOP FT	ΔHnpl FT	Q CFM	V MPH	V FPM
0.45	85	105	36.1	14.0	2.6	1.313	32.2	3.4	18.0	7.3	2,020	1.6	144.8

	FROM MODEL
	USER DATA
	CONSTANT
	CALCULATED

$$Q = 60\ Cd\ A\ K\ (2g\ \Delta Hnpl\ (To - Ti)\ /\ To)^{\wedge}(1/2) \qquad \text{(EQUATION 1)}$$

SOURCE: ASHRAE HANDBOOK OF FUNDAMNETALS 2005, PAGE 27.11

WHERE:

$\quad$ Cd = 0.40 + 0.0025 | Ti - To |$\qquad$ (EQUATION 2)

$\quad$ A = APERTURE AREA RATION, LOWER:UPPER

$\quad$ K = APERTURE AREA RATIO COEFFICIENT (EMPIRICAL), WHERE 'K' IS APPROXIMATELY:

$$K = 1.388 - e^{\wedge}\text{-}A \qquad \text{(EQUATION 3)}$$

SOURCE: FRANÇOIS LÉVY, AIA

ΔHnpl = DISTANCE TO NEUTRAL POINT, ASSUMED TO BE HALF OF ΔZ
T out = TEMPERATURE AT OUTLET (UPPER) APERTURE (USER SUPPLIES VALUE IN °F, AUTOMATICALLY CONVERTED TO °R (RANKINE; °R = °F + 459.67))
T in = TEMPERATURE AT INLET (LOWER) APERTURE (USER SUPPLIES VALUE IN °F, AUTOMATICALLY CONVERTED TO °R (RANKINE; °R = °F + 459.67))
g = GRAVITATIONAL CONSTANT

FIGURE 5.8 The author's thermal chimney calculation worksheet is integrated in the BIM project file to help assess the performance implications of variations of design variables, primarily thermal chimney height and inlet and outlet aperture areas.

▫ The thermal chimneys themselves were adjusted in height and aperture size to achieve a smaller profile while minimizing airflow rate loss, and these variations were iteratively tested with sun studies.

▫ Sun studies and solar animations for the solstices and equinox indicated when and where the thermal chimneys shaded the PV array (Figure 5.9). Climate data suggests that soon after the autumnal equinox, in late October, the building would transition from cooling-load dominated to heating-load dominated. Several configurations of array were tested in this way, and ultimately the array was distributed in three groups of modules to minimize or eliminate shading caused by roof elements and the thermal chimneys throughout most of the year.

Case Study: Boussoleil

Boussoleil is a detached, single-family residence of approximately 2,500 sf (230 m²) of conditioned space, designed by the author and recently completed in rural Central Texas (Figure 5.10). The project is located on a 16-acre (6.5 ha) site

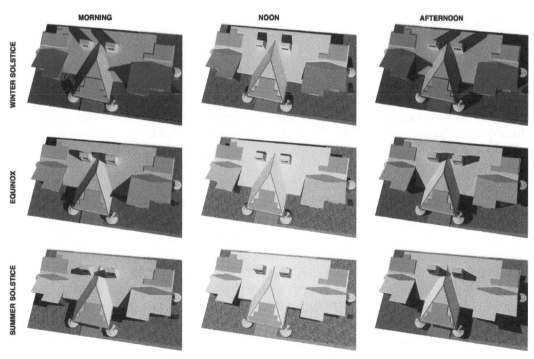

FIGURE 5.9 These sun studies are representative of the types of solar animations undertaken to ensure that various solar chimney configurations being considered would not interfere with photovoltaic collection throughout the year.

FIGURE 5.10 A white "museum board" rendering of the Boussoleil project emphasizing the solar-optimized roof, and curved thermal chimney. A small detached studio and guest cottage is oriented facing true south, top left. This rendering (as well as the others in this case study) was produced by the author using Vectorworks Architect, a BIM-authoring application (see Chapter 2).

with moderate topographical variation and a significant population of mature, indigenous oaks. The project brief required that the home be as energy efficient as possible, with minimal maintenance and operational costs. Minimizing eastern and especially western exposure to control solar heat gain was an appropriate response to local climate. By modeling the earliest design iterations using a BIM authoring tool (Vectorworks Architect), building orientation and roof were optimized to minimize solar heat gain in warm months, while maximizing the potential for onsite solar photovoltaic (PV) energy production. A virtual heliodon tool allowed the generation of a variety of sun studies, both static and animated (Figure 5.11), such that glazed openings could be designed to avoid summer heat gain while still allowing winter solar penetration and passive heating (contrary to popular perception, Texas winters can at times be chilly). Simultaneously, the solar PV array could be located based on sizing assumptions to avoid self-shading

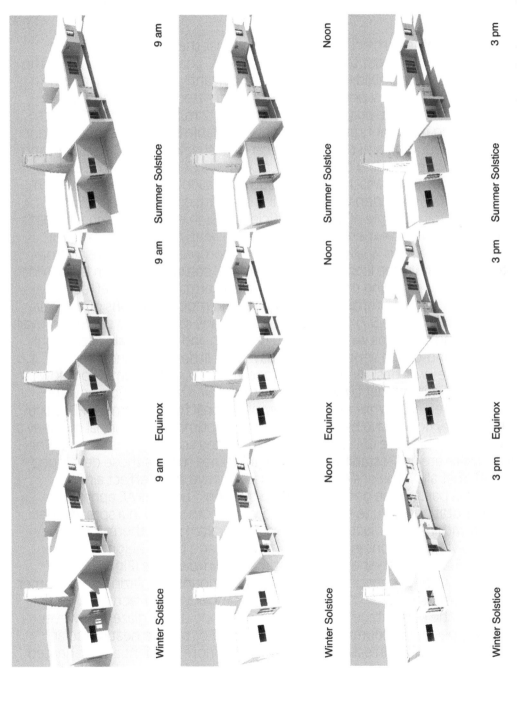

FIGURE 5.11 An early design-development iteration of the Boussoleil project was rendered under a variety of solar conditions in order to optimize glazing placement and roof overhangs.

135

entirely and diminish shading from neighboring trees and ancillary roof structures (chimney, vent stacks, and thermal chimney)—see also Figure 5.15, further on.

Moreover, another project requirement was that the floor be on a single level with no steps, in order to address the owners' goals for aging in place. The ground at the selected building site sloped significantly, and such that a true orientation to the cardinal points would entail increased site work and have a significant portion of the building well over 6 feet (2 m) out of grade. By once again employing the quantitative information available in BIM, a variety of slight variations in orientation and their effects on solar shading could be studied and compared to corresponding cut-and-fill calculations derived from the BIM site model. An azimuth that was 15° east of south represented a balance between minimal loss of PV collection while reducing sitework costs (Figure 5.12).

A fundamental principle of energy-efficient design is to reduce energy loads first, then seek ways to expend energy more efficiently when such expenditures are necessary, and finally to find ways to appropriately generate alternatives to fossil fuels. In the local hot-humid climate, natural ventilation is the most appropriate passive cooling method to increase thermal comfort, effectively extending the human comfort zone to hotter and moister regions of the psychrometric chart (Figure 5.7). The project was already oriented to capture prevailing breezes, and openings were arranged on north and south walls accordingly to maximize wind-driven ventilation. For days with little or no wind, however, a thermal chimney was designed to encourage vertical airflow from a cool, low inlet to the hot, high outlet by means of warming air's natural buoyancy (the so-called stack effect). While intensive computational fluid dynamic (CFD) calculations in theory could have been undertaken to optimize the thermal chimney's performance, in practice CFD tools were beyond the scope of this project. Fortunately, there are well-established design guidelines such as those developed by ASHRAE that allow the designer to estimate passive stack effect air flow rates based in part on the geometry of the building. The ASHRAE approximation is computationally quite tractable, and was incorporated in a spreadsheet embedded within the project BIM file. As a result, alternative thermal chimney designs involving variations in window outlet sizes and tower height could be instantly evaluated for their effect on estimated airflow rates (Figure 5.13).

Architects who are conscious of appropriate amounts of glazing (for summer and winter conditions) may consider a project's window wall fraction (WWF), a measure of the percentage of the vertical envelope that is glazed. However, WWF alone does not account for wall orientation. For passive heating, solar savings fraction (SSF)—an estimate of how much more efficient a solar-heated building is compared to a similar conventionally heated one—may be determined by the ratio of south-facing glass and internal, exposed thermal mass.

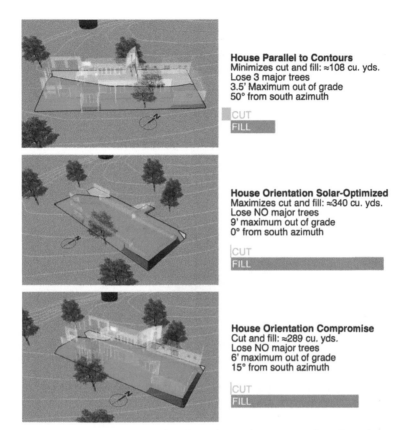

House Parallel to Contours
Minimizes cut and fill: ≈108 cu. yds.
Lose 3 major trees
3.5' Maximum out of grade
50° from south azimuth

CUT
FILL

House Orientation Solar-Optimized
Maximizes cut and fill: ≈340 cu. yds.
Lose NO major trees
9' maximum out of grade
0° from south azimuth

CUT
FILL

House Orientation Compromise
Cut and fill: ≈289 cu. yds.
Lose NO major trees
6' maximum out of grade
15° from south azimuth

CUT
FILL

FIGURE 5.12 Even on a 16-acre (6.5 ha) site there isn't always complete freedom to site a building for optimum photovoltaic collection. These diagrams illustrate the quantitative analysis undertaken to negotiate competing site work concerns—minimizing cut and fill, preserving trees, and maintain an accessible floor plan—without unduly compromising solar shading and PV collection. Here the analytical opportunities of a BIM site model and solar modeling helped satisfy both concerns.

In the case of Boussoleil, BIM was used to dynamically compare the amount of south glazing to the exposed area of adjacent exposed concrete floors and interior brick surfaces (Figure 5.14). As the design evolved, a simple internal worksheet querying the model for the respective material areas automatically provided updated information on the probable SSF. Fenestration and glazing decisions could therefore simultaneously be evaluated for wind-driven ventilation, stack effect ventilation, and summer and winter solar gain, as well as for purely architectural considerations.

The BIM, if materials are appropriately classified, can be queried for a variety of material quantity reports, from gross floor area comparisons to more

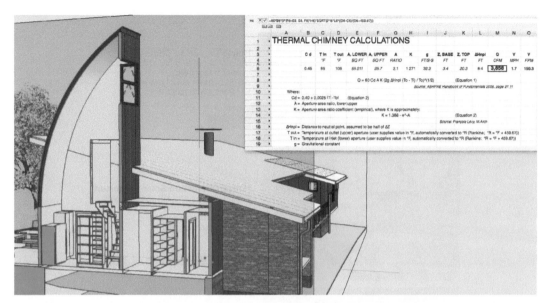

FIGURE 5.13 The thermal chimney's east, south, and west orientations are heavily glazed to encourage heating its upper air, which entrains lower, cooler air as it rises and is exhausted from the south window. The thermal chimney's estimated performance (in terms of volumetric air flow) is calculated based on the geometry inherent to the model and a formula found in the *ASHRAE Handbook of Fundamentals*. While less accurate than a full CFD analysis, such a calculation can help the designer quickly evaluate the relative merits of a variety of design alternatives as tower height and aperture sizes vary.

FIGURE 5.14 South-facing glazed area in the Boussoleil project is compared to accessible internal thermal mass (in the form of exposed concrete flooring and brick fireplace surround) to estimate the design's solar savings fraction.

detailed tabulations of specific wall assembly areas, roofing materials, interior finishes, and of course door and window schedules. Such material takeoffs (Figure 5.15) have a practical value in helping general contractors produce more precise interim cost estimates of probable project costs. In addition, alternative building systems may be evaluated with the objective of reducing material waste. For example, the material costs of wood framing techniques that use larger dimensional lumber spaced at larger intervals (so-called Advanced Framing) may be readily quantitatively compared to more traditional framing techniques. Such comparisons may then be used to evaluate the feasibility of such alternative construction. Similarly, panelized construction systems may be evaluated for a given project by analyzing the quantitative information inherent to BIM.

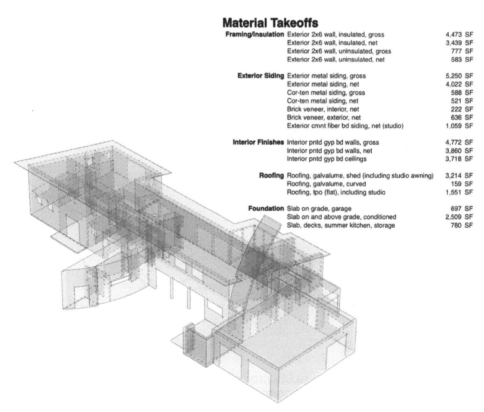

Material Takeoffs

Framing/Insulation	Exterior 2x6 wall, insulated, gross	4,473 SF
	Exterior 2x6 wall, insulated, net	3,439 SF
	Exterior 2x6 wall, uninsulated, gross	777 SF
	Exterior 2x6 wall, uninsulated, net	583 SF
Exterior Siding	Exterior metal siding, gross	5,250 SF
	Exterior metal siding, net	4,022 SF
	Cor-ten metal siding, gross	588 SF
	Cor-ten metal siding, net	521 SF
	Brick veneer, interior, net	222 SF
	Brick veneer, exterior, net	636 SF
	Exterior cmnt fiber bd siding, net (studio)	1,059 SF
Interior Finishes	Interior pntd gyp bd walls, gross	4,772 SF
	Interior pntd gyp bd walls, net	3,860 SF
	Interior pntd gyp bd ceilings	3,718 SF
Roofing	Roofing, galvalume, shed (including studio awning)	3,214 SF
	Roofing, galvalume, curved	159 SF
	Roofing, tpo (flat), including studio	1,551 SF
Foundation	Slab on grade, garage	697 SF
	Slab on and above grade, conditioned	2,509 SF
	Slab, decks, summer kitchen, storage	780 SF

FIGURE 5.15 Another view of the same Boussoleil project file, this one rendered to show solid envelope materials only, alongside the author's material takeoff report generated directly within Vectorworks. As the design evolves, the report is dynamically updated.

Regionally, rural residences have required deeper and deeper water wells over the last two decades, in part because of changing weather patterns but also due to the encroachment of suburban development, which stresses and lowers the water table. For such projects, harvested rainwater has become an increasingly attractive water source, for irrigation as well as for domestic use. While BIM authoring applications do not include a "rainwater harvesting tool," it is possible in most of these applications to dynamically link available projected roof area to user-provided rainfall data in order to size storage cisterns, the single most expensive component of a rainwater system (Figure 5.16). While simple formulas for these calculations pre-date BIM and are readily available, the advantage of including them in the BIM file is that cistern sizing may be determined at any step of the design process. This allows the designer to rapidly weigh the architectural impact on the project of various roof designs and their dependent cisterns.

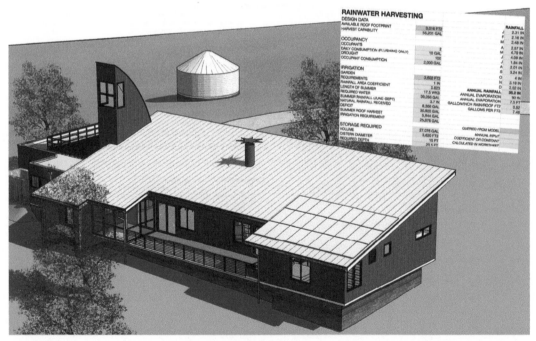

FIGURE 5.16 The roof in the Boussoleil BIM project file is an "intelligent" object, able to report its actual surface area (amount of roofing material) as well as its projected area (footprint in plan view), and distinguishing area over conditioned space from overhangs. Here, a custom worksheet queries the plan projected roof area in order to calculate the required cistern size. Accurate modeling of the building's site, tree canopies, and the elements of the design itself help maximize the PV array's unobstructed solar access.

Case Study: Boardwalk on Lady Bird Lake

The purpose of the Boardwalk is to provide a safe, scenic passage across a 1.3-mile gap in the Hike and Bike Trail stretching from the Austin–American Statesman property to Lakeshore Park along Lady Bird Lake, the geographical center and genius loci of Austin, Texas. It runs on dry land, across open water, through a woodland corridor and across wetlands. Capturing magnificent views of the Austin skyline, it encounters undisturbed natural scenery along secluded limestone bluffs (Figure 5.17). Since opening in June 2014, the Boardwalk has attracted over 750,000 users and garnered local and state design awards.

The project involved an array of considerations: park planning, federal permitting, watershed hydrology, sustainability, and landscape. Mindful of the logistical challenges of building on an ecologically fragile site, the design was intended to be fabricated off-site insofar as possible, then delivered and assembled on-site, thereby speeding construction time and limiting environmental impact. To that end, the structural logic of the Boardwalk is based on a "kit of parts" collection of short-span elements. Galvanized steel and concrete were chosen for their simplicity and durability.

Kit of Parts. In addition to the challenges of the natural site, the project was further complicated by uncertainty surrounding the availability of land on which to locate it. From the beginning, the client (the City of Austin) held the right to place the project in the water, and in addition owned some of but not all the adjoining waterfront. There were opportunities to negotiate the acquisition of some of this private land in order to reduce more expensive construction over open water, but these negotiations would take time to explore and conclude, and injected an element of uncertainty in the project. As land negotiations might extend the project's timeline beyond imposed deadlines, a modular design had the additional virtue of allowing for the design process to move forward, even before the final route was settled.

Because the Boardwalk would transition from land to open water, the design had to accommodate curved radii as an important criterion. A "kit of parts" that could flexibly address straight and curved paths was critical to a successful project (Figure 5.18), even as the route evolved as new land became available and as obstacles, like significant trees or environmental features, were encountered.

The "kit" is a small collection of 20-foot (6 m) trapezoidal spans that—when assembled in series—create all of the straight runs and curves the project required. While this was helpful for planning reasons, it also made construction more manageable. The spanning elements are galvanized steel, and the deck is custom-designed precast planks. The ability to fabricate repetitive elements was crucial to meeting the project schedule and budget.

FIGURE 5.17 Aerial photo of the Boardwalk on Lady Bird Lake in Austin, Texas, with a view of downtown to the northwest and a detail of one of the three shade structures (inset).

Image courtesy of Limbacher & Godfrey Architects, photos by James M. Innes.

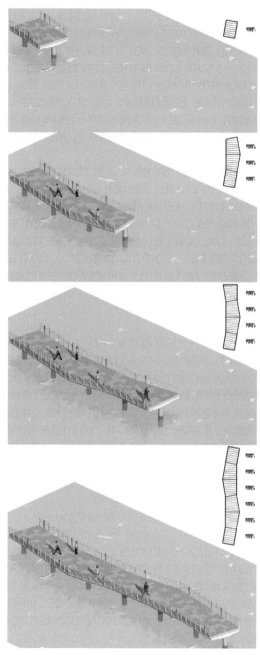

FIGURE 5.18 The conceptual progression of sections of the Boardwalk, each composed of repetitive parts designed to accommodate variation based on orientation.

Image courtesy of Limbacher & Godfrey Architects.

BIM. The multidisciplinary design team was led by a global engineering consultancy. Both the structural and the civil engineers came to the project from a highway engineering background, and were unused to the particulars of architectural detailing. As subconsultants, the architects needed to communicate clearly and efficiently across these and other disciplines, for which BIM was essential. Furthermore, BIM helped communicate with the owner's project management team, facilitating decision making in a fast-moving, very public process. All of the design and detailing was based on a computer-modeling workflow.

Shade. Along its eastern reach, three shade structures were designed to mark observation areas and to create a sense of place. The shade itself was also welcome. Using the "kit of parts" sensibility as a place of beginning, the designs developed as an array of leaves over steel structures composed of off-the-shelf components (Figure 5.19). The complexity of the branching was made simple with BIM, both as a design and as a communication tool. The rich potential for presenting alternative geometries from a variety of perspectives was invaluable to the process.

Case Study: Elgin Residence

Too Much Too Late? Energy modeling is a critical design factor for many projects, even if many smaller buildings would not seem to warrant it for reasons of cost, or its novelty to smaller-scale design workflows. Moreover, proper energy modeling requires detailed inputs on mechanical systems and patterns of occupation; that data may not be available earlier in the design process. By the time that information is available, it may be too late to make significant improvements to the project's performance. This case of too much data too late in the design process may be exacerbated by the tendency to delay verifying energy code compliance until late in the design process. It's a little late to change a wall assembly design just before issuing for permit.

Just as most aspects of building design, envelope energy performance should be considered in schematic design (SD), refined in design development (DD), and detailed in construction documents (CDs). Fortunately, architects have BIM energy *analysis* (as distinct from energy *modeling*) tools at their disposal. Whereas energy modeling implies a comprehensive simulation of thermal performance, energy analysis makes more general, yet valid assumptions and calculations concerning building performance without resorting to full FEA (finite element analysis) of the model.

Commonly available built-in BIM tools like Vectorworks' Energos or ARCHICAD's Energy Evaluation allow the designer to make conceptual energy analyses at early design phases. For example, the architect can stipulate envelope assembly R-values/U-factors as prescriptive targets in SD, then substitute specific wall assemblies for generic ones as the design is developed. Simply by substituting

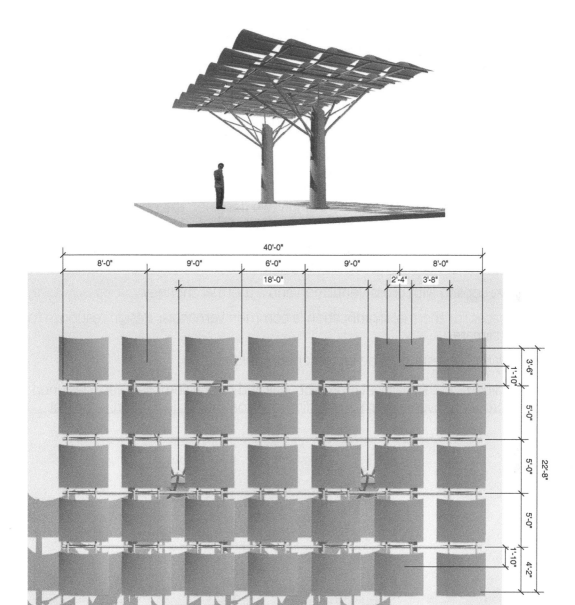

FIGURE 5.19 One of the Boardwalk shade structures BIM models. Models like this one were used to conceive, develop, communicate, and coordinate the design and were key to interacting with the project's engineering team, who employed a largely 2D-only workflow.

Image courtesy of Limbacher & Godfrey Architects.

one wall type for another, competing hypothetical scenarios can be compared and the benefit of a proposed change evaluated. By the time granular energy modeling is deployed, the design has already been vetted at a coarser level, avoiding the pitfall of "too much analysis too late."

Our firm was engaged to design a single-family home in Elgin, Texas (Figure 5.20), a small town outside of Austin. Like many owners these days, our clients were very concerned with the energy performance of their new home, and they possessed a level of physics and engineering knowledge beyond what is typical. Their technical engagement in the design process was unusually high, and that only improved the project as we were challenged to think carefully about all our design decisions. Accordingly, we designed the house with our characteristic concerns for climatic responsiveness:

- Passive orientation, window and roof overhang design based on sun studies to minimize summer and fall solar heat gain.
- Passive cooling with cross-ventilation and a thermal chimney.
- Tall spaces for thermal stratification (a common vernacular design response to Texas climate).
- Rainwater harvesting, to be incrementally phased in.

In addition, on this particular project, wall and roof assemblies were designed with appropriate overall thermal detailing and continuous insulation to defeat

FIGURE 5.20 An architectural rendering of the Elgin Residence.

thermal bridging (Figure 5.21). Designing for thermal breaks requires attention to detail, some additional costs, and careful installation of wall assemblies. Moreover, defeating thermal bridging is increasingly important in energy efficient design, the greater the indoor and outdoor temperature differential. While 105° F (40° C) days in Central Texas' Climate Zone 2 are not uncommon in the summer, that's still a far lesser temperature differential between indoors and outdoors than the 70° F (21° C) or more that you would find on a winter day in, say, Climate Zone 6. Thermal breaks are always good practice in theory, but expensive or exotic details may not always be cost effective in warm or mild climates. As for many of our projects, we used BIM energy analysis to compare envelope performance with and without a thermally broken roof assembly, helping us better inform our client as to the quantifiable impact of implementing additional continuous insulation in the roof. As it turned out, our model showed less than a 1% improvement in roof envelope thermal performance.

While that analysis may not be predictive of real-world performance—neither is energy modeling, incidentally—it does provide a useful and reliable measure by which to validate design decisions. In other words, BIM-embedded energy analysis can help architects weigh the relative merits of alternative design options, and design accordingly.

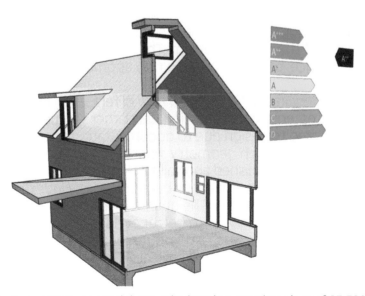

FIGURE 5.21 From our Energos model, we calculated an envelope loss of 25,322 Btu/FT2/year for our roof assembly: metal roofing, open-cell spray foam insulation in the vaulted roof cavity roof and thermal bridging at rafter/decking connections. A similar roof that was thermally broken assembly yielded annual losses of 25,086 Btu/FT2/year—less than a 1% improvement.

Conclusion

In architecture, especially in architectural education, we often refer to "design problems," and that is an apt term. Design problems are often quite complex, and are required to resolve competing agendas of site, climate, context, program, use, aesthetic and architectural concerns, constructibility, permitting, durability, and cost. Indeed, the traditional approach to architectural design is classic problem solving:

◻ Establish a statement of the problem.

◻ Suggest a plausible solution based on experience, training, and best practices.

◻ Investigate the parameters and limitations of any viable solutions.

◻ Iteratively propose progressively refined solutions to balance often competing agendas.

◻ Validate the refined solutions by testing them against the explicit or implicit objectives and feasibility.

Good design solves problems (great design solves them elegantly and beautifully). Like any problem solver, a designer is most successful when good data is available. BIM helps provide that data; not just about the conditions of the design (site restrictions, solar geometry, and so on), but also feedback about the proposed design solution itself. When the designer capitalizes on that opportunity, queries the evolving the model, and weighs the resulting information against other, architectural judgments, then the resulting design is richer and likelier to solve more aspects of the design problem. The designer might rely on intuition informed by experience, but such intuition may at times be faulty, even when well informed.

The process efficiencies that a BIM workflow offers, even in the case of small architectural practices, enable a proportionately larger segment of the design process to be dedicated to design due to documentation time savings. Moreover, the same information-rich geometry inherent to BIM also facilitates the designer's applying well-established and validated quantitative design guidelines to the design. BIM projects may thus be more closely indexed to site conditions, climate, and solar geometry. The quantitative assessment of materials use may likewise permit the designer to better evaluate the effect on resources of competing design solutions. Such a computational design process may lead to better-performing architectural projects. This is especially the case for smaller buildings, for which external energy loads (i.e., climate loads) have a more significant impact on performance than internal ones.

Chapter 6

Case Studies in Digital Fabrication

This chapter exposes projects and project vignettes that point to an intimate relationship between the designing and making of architecture. In these projects, the integration of BIM in the design process was fundamental to resolving design issues within the context of constructability. BIM for constructability is a common theme of "big BIM" (BIM for interoperability and collaboration), and big BIM tends to emphasize documentation coordination and construction. These case studies, on the other hand, are intended to illustrate the recursive nature of BIM for design, considering issues of constructability in the context of informing design processes and outcomes.

Introduction

The phrase *digital fabrication* may bring to mind exotic geometry that blurs or even crosses the line between architecture and purely formal sculpture, science-fiction-inspired images of additive fabrication processes, internationally famed starchitects, or romantic notions of the redemptive social possibilities of the maker/hacker movement. And probably few or none of the above lie within the day-to-day experiences of the majority of practicing architects. Yet in a very real sense, even for the more typical modern architectural practice, the path from the drawing board—or more properly, from the keyboard—to the realized project is potentially quite short.

Pure digital fabrication implies a more or less direct digital path from model to output, even if in reality there may be several steps of postprocessing of data to effect the transition from model geometry and material data to fabrication. A part or assembly may be conceptually developed in a 3D modeling application (whether technically a BIM authoring application or a pure modeler), but manipulation of the data is usually required to produce any kind of output. Moreover, the author must have an understanding of the nature and limitations of the fabrication process. For example, consideration must be given to the wall thickness of a hollow or shelled element. Just as practitioners of traditional architectural design processes need to understand the nature of both the material limitations and the assembly processes of wood, steel, concrete, and so forth, so too must the digital architect understand the kinds of morphologies that digital fabrication can support—or not. Whether 3D printing or CNC routing, usually the process is not simple as issuing a print command from the authoring software. Indeed, the discussion of the relationship between tool, user, and artifact of previous chapters is entirely germane here.

In the interests of being of service to as broad a range of practicing architects and designers as possible, this chapter deliberately casts a wide net. Rather than limit the discussion of digital fabrication to advanced cutting-edge processes, I've included instances of advanced uses of BIM that are integrated in the design process in order to facilitate construction. While groundbreaking work by the likes of Point B Design of Philadelphia is certainly award worthy and may point to a paradigm of future architectural practice, projects like their lyrically constructive D-Bridge lie well outside the norm of most of today's practices. A more expansive paradigm of the relationship between data-rich digital design and construction may encourage more architects to explore greater design freedom, whether applied to structural expressionism, satisfying higher performative standards, or meeting more restrictive construction constraints.

Case Studies

Paired Case Studies: A.GRUPPO Architects' Battle Bend House and Laman Residence

Andrew Nance, AIA, A.GRUPPO Architects, San Marcos, Texas

Constructability and the birth of exotic BIM. In 1994, Neil Denari gave a lecture to architecture students at The University of Texas at Arlington. He was discussing his latest work and presented his recently developed Massey Residence, an exploration of his "World Sheet" concept of a continuous surface wrapped in such a way as to define space. He explained that he had eventually realized that although people were excited about his designs, in order to get them built, he would need to show all the key trades how to do so. His strategy for this project was to digitally construct every structural member and assembly as a "proof of concept." He was very quick to point out that every stud and beam had been modeled and the project depicted to as high a degree of accuracy and "reality" as possible (Figure 6.1). This was just before the arrival of Microsoft Windows 95 and ubiquitous personal computing. Whereas Denari had appropriated modeling software used in Hollywood for special effects and scientific visualizations, we now have BIM. And so over 20 years later, Denari's process still provokes the question: How can what we now call BIM enable buildable, spatially expressive architectures?

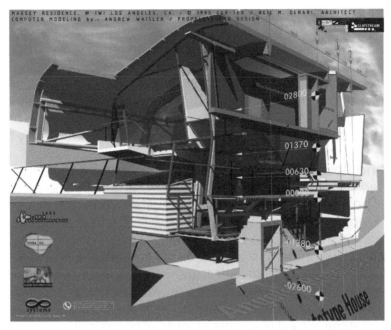

FIGURE 6.1 Sectional perspective with dimension lines of the Massey residence at (W) Los Angeles, CA.

Image created in 1994. Credit: 1995 Cor-Tex / Neil M. Denari Architects.

Structural "underlay." In our firm, we have explored increasingly ambitious spatial conditions, requiring correspondingly challenging structural solutions. As architects, we are not tasked with replacing the structural engineering discipline, but seek to better understand appropriate structural responses to architectural expressions, more closely integrating structural concerns with our practice of architecture. Working with talented structural engineers while gaining a better understanding of best practices for framing assemblies in steel and wood, our evolving integration of increasingly convincing building structural modeling has led us closer to our desired results.

Forensic architectonics. In contrast to a forensic anthropologist who "develops" the final façade of a skull through an understanding of the built-up layers of tissue and bone structure, we explore the process in reverse: taking the façade or skin of the project and working backward to discover a plausible structural solution. The insight that the face/façade is the resultant of its substructure is seemingly obvious, yet has far-reaching implications when evaluating structural systems, whether steel frame, dimensional lumber wood-frame assemblies, panel systems, or monolithic poured plastic materials. Digital modeling has become our primary medium for exploring potential structural solutions and their associated resulting forms. In addition to being an exploratory medium, BIM allows us to effectively communicate our vision with our allies: engineers, fabricators, and installers. We can build cogent and convincing structural arguments and work toward a collaborative solution for structural design and assembly. Leveraging the strength of BIM's visual coordination, we construct diagrams of layered information that is simultaneously subjacent to and superimposed on the architectural model. Moreover, in modeling the sequencing of the architecture and its subtended structure, our concern is not merely formal, but on the sequencing of the assembly of its parts.

Battle Bend House. The projects shown here illustrate the value of a modeled integrated structure approach to architectural design. The Battle Bend House is four-bedroom residence located in Austin, Texas, and was conceived as a kind of double courtyard house: a front "public" and a rear "private" space is defined by an "L" shape plan set back from the road. Commissioned as a speculative property development, it was the first new construction in a "custom home" neighborhood in three decades. It is thus modestly scaled and takes cues from the neighboring 1970s ranch homes. Stylistic elements such as gable roof and shed dormers found in the neighboring residences were transformed into space-defining architectural elements at interior conditions.

Being a one-level residence, the ceiling plane manipulation was a key contributor to the spatial experiences of the building. Dynamic spatial expression was achieved through the intersection of the simple vaulted gable roof and shed dormers glazed with translucent walls. The resulting ceiling plane at the intersections of the vaulted roof and shed dormers became sculptural expression as we became very interested in articulating the ceiling plane and resulting forms.

Its composition of volumetrically explicit gables devoid of tension members or "rafter ties" is organized around a loose courtyard and complemented by two sets of tall glazed dormers or light monitors. To address the roof thrusts that we intuitively understood would occur, we developed a series of shear walls to offset those forces. These shear walls were not afterthoughts introduced late in design by our consulting structural engineer but were explicitly modeled in design, integral to the architectural expression of the project, and carefully diagrammed as part of the design process (Figure 6.2). They are essential to the architectural character of the spaces (Figures 6.3 and 6.4).

The resulting structural solution of dropped beams, transfer girders, and shear walls allowed for standardized "stick" construction and were carefully developed to cleanly articulate the open spaces and clean lines desired.

Laman Residence. In the Laman Residence, a modified gambrel roof structure without tension members at the roof spring point required an alternative mechanism to overcome thrust. Here again, explicitly addressing structural

FIGURE 6.2 Section through living room and glazed dormer showing folded roof/ceiling planes. The light monitor filters light through a relatively narrow aperture, flooding the adjacent living room from above.

Image courtesy of Andrew Nance, AIA, A.GRUPPO Architects.

FIGURE 6.3 Vignettes of light monitor / glazed dormers at master closet (left) and guest room (right). The articulation of the ceiling planes at the intersection of the light monitors and glazed dormers results in a sculptural expression and varied spatial conditions.

Image courtesy of Andrew Nance, AIA, A.GRUPPO Architects.

issues early in the design led us to a richer architectural expression. A series of baffle walls provides both structural resolution to static forces and a sensual mitigation of the defining clerestory's potentially intense natural light. Procedurally, we began the Design Development phase by assembling a structural model, digitally preassembling the building with Vectorworks ARCHITECT's wall and roof framing tools. In addition to uncovering new opportunities for architecture, that model served to solicit preliminary proposals for structural design.

Upon retirement after 40 years of teaching Fiber Arts and Interior Design, the clients desired a gallery and studio addition to complement their 1970s-era modern home. Over the past 30 years, the Lamans had created a series of outdoor rooms and gardens around their home, leaving the front as the only viable area for an addition. As artists, the owners were interested in the addition comprising bold, sculptural forms. Characterized by paired towers (gallery and studio) flanking a foyer with an upper-level library, the addition had the rare opportunity to reinvent the facade of the residence. In early studies it became apparent that in thinking of the exterior as an extruded "shell," several opportunities arose to define uniquely sculptural interior spaces. Combined with a passive and active natural lighting strategy, a series of rich and varied spatial conditions were achieved.

Structurally insulated panels (SIPs) seemed well suited to the structural task of creating this literal "shell" composed of diaphanous plans. The design team

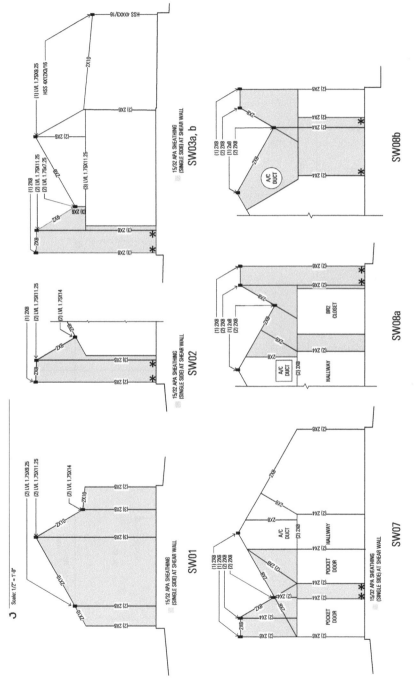

FIGURE 6.4 To address the roof thrusts that we intuitively understood would occur, we developed a series of shear walls to offset those forces. These shear walls were not afterthoughts introduced late in design by our consulting structural engineer but were explicitly modeled in design, integral to the architectural expression of the project, and carefully diagrammed as part of the design process.

Image courtesy of Andrew Nance, AIA, A.GRUPPO Architects.

155

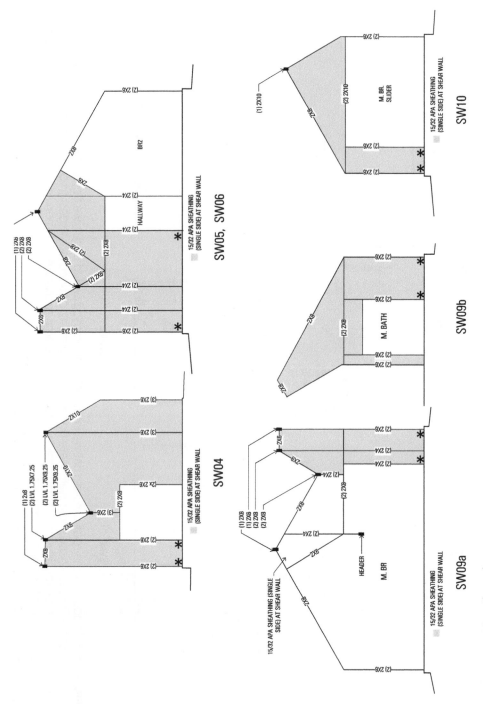

FIGURE 6.4 (*Continued*)

included two structural engineers and a SIPs manufacturer (GeoFaze of Kerrville, Texas) to develop a strategy for fabricating and assembling the SIPs.

The BIM model was exported to GeoFaze, who then used their proprietary SIPs software to create the fabrication model. Their model, reflecting their fabrication capabilities, was then overlaid on the architectural model to verify accuracy and identify any areas for revision—either in the design or fabrication. The models were then used to choreograph the order of SIPs delivery and assembly on site (Figure 6.5).

The most challenging areas for fabrication and assembly was the "bent" wall condition, where the wall transforms to the roof plane. It was desired to avoid tension ties or cross members to maintain the clarity of form of the space. In response, the SIPS structural engineer developed a bent-column constructed out of engineered lumber, sandwiched between the panels, designed to resist the outward thrust at the bend (Figure 6.6).

The natural lighting strategy was realized in two ways: a glazed north wall of the towers provides even and diffused light throughout the day, while a series of skylights provides direct lighting that changes with the sun position. In an attempt to accentuate the direct lighting scheme, a series of baffles was introduced at the ceiling plane to capture and reflect the natural light. The warm contrast of direct light offers a dynamic contrast to the cool, even lighting of the north-facing glazed walls, providing a unique character of lighting that changes constantly. These baffles, integral to the lighting scheme, simultaneously serve as collar ties at the peak. Only half were required for structural reasons, but all were necessary to achieve the desired lighting effects (Figure 6.7).

Case Study: San Saba

This unbuilt project was an effort to express a simple plan in a rural, open landscape. The austere internal arrangement of the house was surrounded and defined by a three-sided porch, providing shade to generous outdoor spaces appropriating an expansive site, a modest cattle ranch. The pitch of each roof face, oriented in a cardinal direction, varied according to the depth of the porch in that particular direction (Figure 6.8). Supporting the porch was a colonnade of double steel columns: pairs of bent hot-dipped galvanized C-channels formed Y-like yokes to support the steel-flitched wood porch perimeter beams. Each steel member of the pair was identical, but rotated 180° relative to its twin, in order to achieve the distinguishing yoke profile (Figure 6.9, left). Pairs of double columns stood off from the direct outside corners at three of the porch's four corners, such that the supported beams were cantilevered at the corners (Figure 6.9, right).

The structural conditions at the corners created substantial forces, and the consulting engineer's preliminary assessment suggested steel hip beams would

FIGURE 6.5 The BIM model was used to verify the fabrication model supplied by the manufacturer as well as in visualizing the sequence of construction.

Image courtesy of Andrew Nance, AIA, A.GRUPPO Architects.

FIGURE 6.6 Bent columns were fabricated from engineered lumber sandwiched by a pair of steel plates to counteract outward thrust at the roof's "spring point," resulting in sculpted interior space.

Image courtesy of Andrew Nance, AIA, A.GRUPPO Architects.

FIGURE 6.7 The light baffles have a dual role as collar tie and reflecting the light admitted from the skylights above.

Image courtesy of Andrew Nance, AIA, A.GRUPPO Architects.

be required at all three open porch corners (the position of the garage to the northwest afforded a continuous structural wall and no open corner). As an alternative to full steel beams, glue-laminated hip beams were designed with a modified, tapered wide-flange steel connections where they met the cantilevered porch beams. Due to the variable roof pitches and a constant perimeter

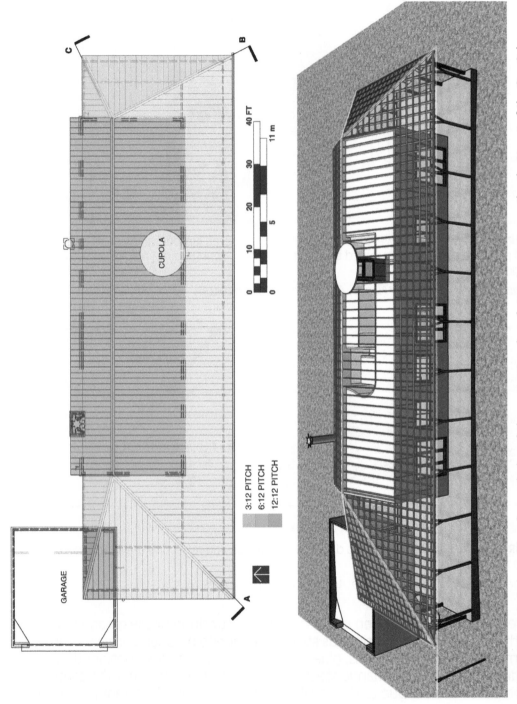

GARAGE

CUPOLA

3:12 PITCH
6:12 PITCH
12:12 PITCH

0   10   20   30   40 FT

0   5   11 m

FIGURE 6.8 A roof plan with color-coded roof slopes (top) and roof structure perspective (bottom) of the San Saba project. Note that in the plan the porch areas under roof are a lighter shade than the conditioned central core of the house. Detail keys A, B, and C refer to Figure 6.10.

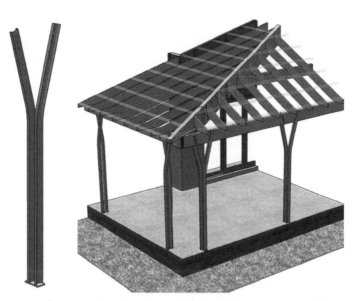

FIGURE 6.9 A rendering of one of the San Saba "yoke" bent steel channel double columns (left) and a roof structure detail of the BIM model. Each half of the column is identical. The roofing is not shown and the roof purlins are rendered transparent for clarity.

beam, the ends of the hip beams would have a pronounced taper, resulting in a profile for which steel was a suitable material.

Steel is, however, a more expensive and far less forgiving material than wood; adjustments to the shape or geometry of the hip beam ends could not readily be made in the field once formed. For a simple truss gang plate or angle connection, the disparate scheduling of steel and wood is not usually a problem. Here, the design was a little less straightforward. Moreover, the steel would have to be fabricated long before the wood framing to which it would connect would be in place, so the framing would have to accurately conform to the construction documents, with little or no deviation. It was therefore crucial that the engineering (and eventually steel shop drawings) be as accurate as possible.

In early schematic design, the roof was modeled at a conceptual level using Vectorworks ARCHITECT's Roof tool, testing various porch depths and roof face pitches until a suitable architecture was resolved. (In a parametric BIM tool like the roof, individual roof faces can vary in pitch, bearing height, and overhang within a given roof assembly). Later in the design process, the roof model geometry was analyzed by Vectorworks Roof Framer, and individual roof members (perimeter beams, rafters, hip beams, and purlins) were automatically modeled based on the parameters provided. The actual structural analysis was performed by the consulting engineer, whereupon the roof member sizes were updated in the model to reflect the structural design based on load calculations.

For the hip beam connections, the architectural BIM was updated based on structural sketches provided by the engineer. Since the hip beams were angled in plan, and in two out of three cases negotiate two differently pitched roof faces, each beam's elevation angle (slope) had to be individually adjusted to fit the geometry of the overall roof. The beam end connections were accurately modeled to account for engineered web and flange thicknesses, roof slope, and taper, and even included preliminary bolt patterns based on first-order structural assumptions. Elevation views perpendicular to each beam face were taken, and the architecturally modeled beam end connections were then shared with the structural engineer for approval (Figure 6.10). The consulting engineer refined the load and shear calculations, adjusting the preliminary design appropriately, and specified an updated bolting pattern. These structural details—shared with the author as 2D DWG drawings—were the basis for an updated architectural model to help ensure proper fit and integrity of the design intent, and integration with the roofing system and gutter requirements.

Case Study: GRO Architects Academy Street Microhousing

Richard Garber, AIA GRO Architects, PLLC, New York

Microhousing is not a new concept, but is currently enjoying a great deal of interest in urban US markets. The concept is simple enough: individual dwelling units are designed to be as small and efficient as possible, while the common amenities are larger than those found in typical residential apartment buildings, including gyms, collaborative work spaces, and multipurpose lounges. These amenity spaces allow for greater social interaction within the buildings, fostering a closer community. Compactness allows for densities that are ultimately more sustainable than typical apartment buildings, as building services are provided to more people over the same size footprint. Another important aspect of microhousing is its location within the city. Especially on the East Coast, with its fairly robust transit systems, these projects are sited in areas where multinodal transit opportunities such as subway, bus, and light-rail are available and the use of the automobile is diminished. As such, many microhousing proposals do not contain parking spaces for residents, favoring car-share scenarios or bicycle rooms.

It is important to ground this interest in broader technological shifts of the time. Peter Cachola Schmal, director of the Deutsches Architekturmuseum in Frankfurt, has linked the interest in the capsule, or unit, to the technologies that allowed for the possibility of space travel in the 1960s. "A cosmonaut complete with his life-supporting system had no problem fitting into the first Russian capsules with their 7'-6" diameter. In this time of enthusiasm for technology, the

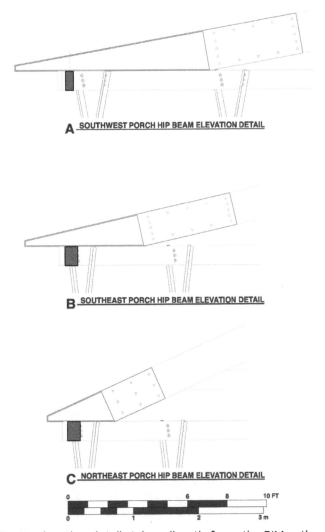

FIGURE 6.10 Architect's elevation details taken directly from the BIM authoring file of the three hip beam end conditions. The steel beam end elements are drawn in red. Each detail (A, B, C) is keyed to the roof plan, top of Figure 6.8.

space capsule was seen as a symbol of progress—a small oasis of human civilization underway to distant worlds, a sort of hypermodern car in space. Their form greatly influenced architects and designers."

The microhousing movement in the United States is firmly rooted in the urban Pacific Northwest. At the time of writing, there are some 780 microunits currently in Seattle, with another 1,600 slated for construction. The units, most of which are between 200 and 300 sf, are attractive because of lower rents and their location in prominent urban centers. City officials tend to be welcoming of microapartments, citing their commonality in Japan and European cities, and their location in walkable urban centers in contrast to sprawl. This type of density is often seen as sustainable, concentrating people where they can readily access building and community services while decreasing their reliance on automobiles. As Susan Kelleher writes in *Pacific NW Magazine*, "Tiny apartments are hardly a new thing, but they've attracted attention and controversy" in Seattle "because developers have been building them at a quick clip—sometimes over the objections of neighbors—and filling them quickly with people seeking rents that match their circumstances and mobile lifestyles."

For Nest Micro Apartments in Jersey City, New Jersey, GRO's microunit project (Figure 6.11), the site is located in the dense Journal Square neighborhood of

FIGURE 6.11 Nest Micro Apartments, Jersey City, New Jersey. Nest Micro Apartments is a new 122-unit building planned in the Journal Square section of Jersey City. The building will contain fully furnished studios as well as amenities in a mass transit–oriented part of the city.

Image courtesy GRO Architects.

the city adjacent to a transit hub that supports NJ Transit buses, taxis, and the Newark–New York PATH train. The project's site is 91'-5" (27.9 m) wide and 100' (30.5 m) deep, and its massing is controlled by the Journal Square Redevelopment Plan, limiting density only by bulk and height standards. The building developers market the units as being for the "millions of young and middle-earning New Yorkers who contribute to their city in so many ways but can't afford their own place in Manhattan."

The project imagines 122 residential units, each ranging between 200 and 280 sf each. An intensive discussion was had with representatives with the New Jersey Department of Community Affairs, which regulates building codes and standards in the state, to ensure that the units met all building and accessibility standards, with the design of the units themselves coming first to ensure feasibility prior to the overall building mass, which was controlled by the redevelopment plan.

The basic unit is designed for a single occupancy with the standard unit module being 11'-0" (3.35 m) wide and 20'-0" (6.1 m) deep. The module is subdivided into a "wet zone," which is 9'-0" (2.74 m) × 11'-0" (3.35 m), and a "dry zone," which is 11'-0" (3.35 m) × 11'-0" (3.35 m). The wet zone, positioned at the unit's interior, contains the requisite accessible bathroom fixtures: shower, toilet, and vanity. However, these are organized individually within the space, with accessibility constraints measured to fixture as opposed to grouping them into a stand-alone bathroom. The occupant enters through this zone, which has individual rooms dedicated for the toilet and shower grouped on one wall. The sink and storage closets line the opposite wall.

The "dry zone" contains a kitchen area with sink and refrigerator as well as a two-burner cooktop and a convection microwave mounted above, and a living area with a foldout couch for sleeping, ample storage, and a small fold-down desk. For the interior design, we worked closely with an Italian furniture manufacturer on a series of space-saving pieces that would be installed in the units during construction (Figure 6.12). All units would be rented as furnished, the concept being that occupants need only to arrive with their clothing and a laptop.

Taking advantage of their position on the street, the south-facing units at the front facade each contain an upholstered cantilevered window box that can accommodate two seated people (Figure 6.13). The window boxes contain a high awning window for ventilation, as well as an operable casement window and a horizontal shade that is calibrated with the building site to allow winter sun to penetrate deep into the units while shading the more intense summer sun. Solar path and angle throughout the year were simulated so as to best understand the optimal length of the shade, which is 12" (305 mm).

FIGURE 6.12 Nest Micro Apartments, Jersey City, New Jersey. The design of the units is more likened to a yacht interior rather than a conventional apartment—surfaces and furniture fold out of walls based on use of the occupant.

Image courtesy GRO Architects.

FIGURE 6.13 Nest Micro Apartments, Jersey City, New Jersey. GRO developed a comprehensive virtual model, adding both 2D and 3D information from engineering consultants. With the small unit sizes (220 sf or 20.4 m²) the model proved to be critical for both trade and scope coordination as well as costing and spatial conflict checking. The south-facing units all feature window boxes that expand the space in the units.

Image courtesy GRO Architects.

Design, BIM, and trade coordination. A dense project brings with it some challenges beyond those of more standard types of residential buildings. First, there is generally a higher degree of coordination required across the design and construction team due to the size of units. If an average one-bedroom apartment containing a bathroom and kitchen is 800–900 sf (74 to 84 m²), then there are four times this amount of plumbing and gas risers, equipment, and fixtures within the same area occupied by four microapartments. In many instances the mechanical, electrical, and plumbing (MEP) consultant will show this information as single lines. Here, however, it was decided that all plumbing and gas runs would be modeled three dimensionally and integrated with the architectural and structural scope to avoid any spatial conflicts between trades. In fact, the BIM file is continuously reviewed with various subcontractors to ensure that each scope is properly coordinated. For Nest, the BIM model is specifically used in trade coordination as well as in the tagging of metadata for the furniture, fixture, and equipment (FFE) package. It is critical that all furniture and equipment practically fit in the units, making them more akin to a yacht interior than a typical apartment. Thus BIM insured that the design is not only novel, but that nearly every square inch is utilized.

Case Study: Big Wheel Burger's Cross-Discipline Design

Neil Barman, Intern Architect AIBC, LEED AP, Barman+Smart Design Services

This project was a tenant improvement within an existing building (see Figure 6.14). It established a second location and commissary kitchen, for a Victoria, BC, Canada, restaurant chain that specializes in ethically produced fast food created from locally sourced ingredients. As part of the restaurant's mandate, the client desired an aesthetic of simple, unpretentious materials within functional spaces.

Restaurant design is a uniquely complex process where the goal is to create something of a "machine" that is made up of rather different but interdependent parts. Kitchen equipment tends to be fairly heavy duty, quite demanding in its size and mechanical requirements, and is dedicated to specific food-prep or storage tasks. On the other hand, the dining area's components tend to be lighter duty, more pleasing to look at or to be with and are meant to create a convenient or comfortable environment for patrons.

The various users of that machine also require it to serve them in different ways. Patrons need a pleasant space to enjoy their food and time spent with each other, staff need a space that aids them in doing their job well and pleases patrons, and owners need a space that effectively represents their brand and maximizes profits. With all of these requirements, BIM can play a significant role, not only in terms of making sure the restaurant machine works and equipment

FIGURE 6.14 A photo of the completed Big Wheel Burger restaurant and commissary kitchen, Victoria, BC, Canada.

Image credit: Neil Barman, Barman+Smart.

details and counts are tracked, but also that it is an appealing place to visit and to work.

Dealing with an existing space meant that the desired program, equipment, and environment had to be accommodated within a preestablished building shell. The majority of the desired kitchen equipment and workflows were well known by the owner and chef and had to be made to work within the space. The HVAC equipment needed to support the kitchen's equipment, and workflows were initially designed very simply to fit within the existing conditions with the understanding that changes may need to occur to have it work with the kitchen's design. Heating, cooling, ventilation, and service connections were designed by a skilled mechanical engineer with a wealth of restaurant expertise to meet the requirements of the equipment, occupancy, and relevant local and provincial building codes as well as to create a comfortable, functional space.

The mechanical engineer provided preliminary specifications and 2D line drawings of the HVAC system as DWG files and equipment cut sheets. We then modeled this equipment in 3D with Vectorworks ARCHITECT, using both a kit of built-in parametric MEP parts and freeform modeling. It became clear early on that the mechanical system's placement within the kitchen space would be an intricate balancing act. During the year prior to our client's acquiring their space, a neighboring establishment had done an extensive renovation and had occupied all of the building's available roof-top area for their own mechanical units. The resulting challenge for us was that we were required to accommodate all of Big Wheel's mechanical equipment within their leased space. The considerable size of the make-up air and heating units, exhaust hood, and cooling compressor made modeling these units in 3D essential to finding their fit in the kitchen. Due to existing building conditions there was limited space for and access to possible duct runs, so modeling ducts again helped determine the feasibility of the technical system The T-bar ceiling design impacted the resulting availability of storage space in the kitchen. Once modeled, the client could see how much space the units would require and how the kitchen would work and feel, and the builder could plan for delivery and installation of the units.

As some of the HVAC's ductwork also extended into the dining area to provide necessary ventilation and air conditioning, the design team could see that this ductwork would need to be considered as part of the interior design. Instead of treating the highly prominent HVAC components as an obstruction to the space's design, we treated it as a design element in its own right with its size, shape, materiality, location, path, and spatial presence being considered in addition to its mere function. The mechanical engineer, who was quite open to feedback on his work, appreciated seeing 3D views of his proposed equipment modeled in the space. Being able to discuss HVAC equipment placement while together viewing live 3D sections of the space, using Vectorworks' Clip Cube, was invaluable for fine tuning both the mechanical equipment and the kitchen's working spaces (Figure 6.15).

While the design team ironed out the kitchen area requirements, the public spaces—entry and ordering, circulation, seating, washrooms—were also being allocated and beginning to taking shape. In keeping with the restaurant's unpretentious character, we designed concrete pony walls to delineate seating areas from traffic areas, and proposed using raw wood and stainless steel for the material palette of built-in cabinetry to further the aesthetic agenda.

With these decisions in place, we provided simple, sketch-style renderings of 3D views to the client and the rest of the team to communicate our design intentions from key vantage points. We intentionally left materials and textures out of some of these initial views in order to have the team focus on the

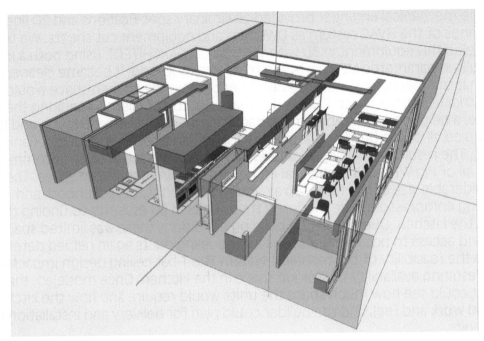

FIGURE 6.15 A live section of the BIM model showing color-coded mechanical equipment, kitchen equipment, and wall layout.

Image credit: Neil Barman, Barman+Smart.

actual spaces themselves. When we presented progress to the client during the design's development, we navigated through the live 3D model in perspective. This method saved the client from having to read and synthesize flat, 2D drawings (Figure 6.16) and instead showed them how their equipment and decisions would be incorporated, or could not be incorporated, into the space with easily comprehensible views (Figure 6.17). This kind of presentation and collaboration method saved considerable design and communication time by providing answers to many of the client's questions in real time.

In turn, the interior designer took cues from the exposed mechanical systems and initial materials palette, creating a playful geometric ceiling "frame" and related bulkhead enclosure as well as making informed light fixture choices. Working from our 2D drawings as well as 3D views, he provided us with sketches of his bulkhead pattern concepts and possible layouts of the ceiling frame. In short time we added these elements in 3D to test their suitability to the design and assess their buildability. During subsequent meetings with the interior designer, we again navigated the 3D model together and made changes "live" in real time. This again avoided the considerable communication time that would

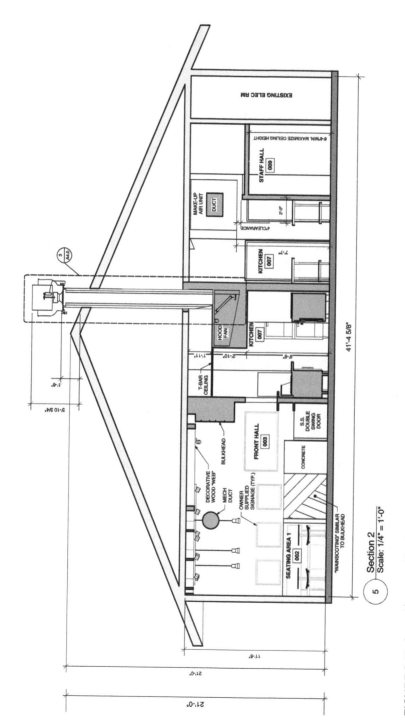

FIGURE 6.16 An orthogonal building section from the BIM file used directly in construction documents (CDs).
Image credit: Neil Barman, Barman+Smart.

FIGURE 6.17 Simple yet effective, relatively basic demonstrations from live BIM models on a laptop can make for compelling presentations to clearly and effectively communicate design proposals to clients, builders, and trades.

Image credit: Neil Barman, Barman+Smart.

have been needed had we been making changes in isolation, sending them to the interior designer for review and waiting for his responses.

Even as early concepts, these elements were incorporated into the 3D model such that all consultants could see and discuss their scopes, discuss each other's work and coordinate construction with the builder. This allowed for design iterations of the ceiling frame to be explored, trying out various options for its extent, pattern, and construction possibilities (Figure 6.18). The design team had a similar exploration of the raw wood-clad lighting bulkhead, and as a result we brought the electrical contractor into the design conversation. Having both of these interior design elements incorporated into the model, combined with the HVAC equipment, facilitated informed, cross-discipline design discussions among the consultants. For example, at one point while navigating the 3D model with these elements in place, it was discovered that proposed ductwork would obstruct sight lines within the restaurant and prevent patrons from seeing menu boards. Having an accurate and comprehensive BIM at hand allowed for views to be explored, facilitated conversations between the mechanical engineer, designer, and clients such that an elegant and visually pleasing solution could be smoothly developed at the design stage, rather than during construction.

This rich collaboration in design development would not have been possible had individual consultants been working independently on their own scopes within their own "silos" of project design and documentation. Moreover—and

FIGURE 6.18 A comparison of an artistic rendering in the BIM authoring software shared with the interior designer (above), and the completed interior public space (below).

Image credit: Neil Barman, Barman+Smart.

this is key—collaboration on this project was a simultaneous and parallel process, rather than being a serial "assembly line" of architecture, followed by MEP design, followed by interior design, all hastily coordinated and reconciled at the end. This deeper type of collaboration also meant that few "surprises" were discovered and had to be solved during the construction phase.

From the client's perspective, having a model available early in the process and developed in conjunction with the various consultants' input into the project allowed them to see where their resources would be spent and what their patrons would experience. The client wasn't expected solely to read 2D drawings to understand how others were realizing their project, and instead was provided an accessible and easy-to-experience model.

Chapter 7

BIM Tomorrow: Trends in Technology

Jeffrey W. Ouellette

Assoc. AIA, IES, AEC Technology Consultant

Advanced technologies are being applied to BIM design processes, expanding the scope and role of digital design. Insights from industry experts illustrate ways that these technologies can enhance rather than hinder the creative process, as much as they contribute to efficient project delivery. In many ways, current implementations are in their infancy, leaving room to speculate on the future impact of these and other technologies as they mature.

A Technology-Rich Future for the Profession

Design is a complex human endeavor mixing objective criteria and subjective values of logic and aesthetics. The number and types of tools available to the designer and the design process are increasing at an astonishing pace, ranging from modeling to simulation and analysis, to prototyping through various 3D printing methods.

Most of these are not so much contemporaneously revolutionary technologies as old technologies that have eventually trickled down to the market. A given technology can penetrate the broader market once it has crossed significant barriers of cost, performance, and user interface. Adoption prior to these breakthroughs is generally prohibitive except for researchers or well-funded practitioners on the bleeding edge. Moreover, the building industry as a whole has traditionally been entrenched. We are very slow to adopt new methodologies and technologies, particularly those that are highly disruptive: perceived to displace skills and knowledge rather than merely enhance productivity and improve profit margins. This is especially true if the investment in adoption appears to be too costly and risky. For this and other reasons, the building industry has fallen behind many others in the innovation and adoption of technology (see Agarwal, Chandrasekaran, and Sridhar's June 2016 article at McKinsey .com, "Imagining Construction's Digital Future").

In spite of that, we may have reached a significant tipping point in the volume of technology and pace at which it is being introduced and adopted. Perhaps now more than ever, new and meaningful opportunities for designers are emerging and seem ripe for exploitation. While a great number of ideas and processes are having effects across the entire spectrum of building design, construction and operations, we'll focus on a few trends that impact the design process:

◻ Digital realities: virtual, augmented, and mixed modes

◻ Computational design and visual programming languages (VPLs)

◻ LiDAR, photogrammetry, and point clouds

◻ Artificial intelligence (AI)

Rather than being mere stand-alone novelties, these technologies are applicable to various BIM-based design processes, with the potential for leveraging the designer's efforts, in addition to increasing efficiencies while adding value to the overall project.

Digital Realities: Virtual, Augmented, and Mixed Modes

With the construction of a 3D model in an infinite and infinitely scalable digital space, there is the opportunity to explore the resulting construct in a variety of immersive visualization modes (Figure 7.1). These modes vary in abstraction from the completely projected virtual environment to an augmentation of the physical environment we experience every day.

The aspiration of inhabiting another reality, like plunging into one's own lucid dream, has captivated artists and visionaries for ages. For most of known architectural history, scale models have been used to extract the ideas from the designer's mind in a visual or tactile form to explore and explain the spaces and structures being considered for construction and habitation (Figures 7.2 and 7.3). Such models can present a new reality to the future inhabitant as well as the designer, imparting a sense of the prospective design before committing to its execution. Yet even with low-tech, if ingenious, methods of immersing one's viewpoint in these vignettes using periscopes, cutouts, and dioramas, these scale models and projections have always been limited, often functioning only from a single perspective.

The pursuit of immersing a viewer into a digital constructed scene has been around as long as computer-generated imagery (CGI). Attempts to inhabit a digital virtual reality have always been hampered by the technical limits of the CGI realm itself, and the ability to create sufficiently realistic 3D geometry, lighting, coloring, textures, and motion has been constrained by available software and hardware.

FIGURE 7.1 A future for BIM. In her master's thesis at the USC School of Architecture, "Virtual Reality Interactivity and the Internet of Things," Lingyan Yu explored and experimented with the use of virtually controlled devices in a BIM environment. In this case, a model vehicle incorporating temperature and humidity sensors was VR-controlled to give real-world environmental data of a virtual space (Karen Kensek, chair of thesis committee).

Virtual reality (VR) is the immersion in a completely digital environment, to the same perceptual scale as the viewer, yet completely removed from the real world (Figure 7.4). It is most often used to represent extensive constructs that do not currently exist and requires a great deal of geometric, textural, and lighting data and processing to portray a desired scene. Most often, VR is experienced

FIGURES 7.2 AND 7.3 For centuries, architects have sought to simulate environments before building them, creating "virtual environments" to evaluate or communicate their designs. The Great Model of Christopher Wren's St. Paul's Cathedral in London was made by William Cleere in 1673–1674, as a record of the architect's design intent beyond what could be communicated in drawings, and to serve as permanent record of the design. Even in recent times models serve as useful virtualization tools, as in the case of the Texas State Capitol Dome model on display at Capitol Visitor's Center in Austin, Texas.

Photo of St. Paul's courtesy of Anne-Marie Nankivell, thelondonphile.com; photo of Texas State Capitol Dome model courtesy of Chloé Lévy.

through the use of dedicated headset hardware that delivers the imagery to the viewer while completely obscuring the surrounding real-world environment. The most well-known include the higher end and tethered devices such as the HTC Vive, Oculus Rift, and Sony PlayStation VR, to the lower end solutions that incorporate the use of a mobile (smart phone) device, such as the many cardboard holders, Google Daydream View, and Samsung Gear VR, among many others. The VR hardware may include manual controllers to enable navigation in the environment beyond simple stationary viewing. The most common VR experience for people involves digital video games, but VR is quickly gaining ground in scientific and medical communities for objectives ranging from simulating

FIGURES 7.2 AND 7.3 *(Continued)*

and investigating molecular structures, to treating post-traumatic stress disorder (PTSD).

As opposed to VR, **augmented reality (AR)** is meant to weave our daily experience of the world with digital constructs that supplement our perceptions with additional information, further enriching our experience. Today, AR is usually experienced through the use of mobile devices with cameras, such as smartphones and tablets, utilizing specialized software to inject, or overlay, the digital information in the device's field of view and resulting display (Figure 7.5). Mobile applications like the Pokémon Go game, Google Translate and SkyMap, Amikasa, and even Snapchat provide consumers with various levels of overlaid contextual information and interactivity. On the higher end, dedicated headset devices similar to VR hardware allow a hands-free approach; such devices include Google Glass, Microsoft Hololens, and DAQRI Smart Glasses and Smart Helmet. These are typically coupled with more specialized software, usually more focused on

FIGURE 7.4 Interior living spaces of two Ray and Charles Eames homes viewed in a VR headset, with realistic renderings above and false-color illuminance levels below.

Image courtesy of Xuanhong Liu and Yu Qi Zhang, USC architecture students for work in Professor Karen Kensek's "Digital Tools for Architecture" course.

FIGURE 7.5 An AR (augmented reality) model viewed on a handheld device, using a set of drawings as a model "base."

Architecturel model and photo by François Lévy, Lévy Kohlhaas Architects.

industrial-, medical-, military-, and business-related applications. These benefit from contextual line-of-sight information delivery, like assembly instructions, maps or way finding indicators, and even replication of computer screen output simply floating in space or projected on desired line-of-sight surfaces.

The newest trend in digital representation is the idea of **mixed, or merged, reality (MR)**, also sometimes known as hybrid (HR) or expanded reality (XR), where the lines of VR and AR are blurred, exploiting a higher degree of inter-activity with data and virtual elements, blended with real physical elements to create a completely new experience (see Figure 7.6). There are varying levels of interactivity, usually with prompts or virtual objects that behave as if responding to the real world context and environment into which they have been inserted. A step or two beyond AR, MR's objects attempt to match the proper perspec-tive view of the real environment with correct location, scale, and even physics, so the virtual objects look and behave as if they are there. MR often utilizes the same simple or sophisticated display hardware used for AR, but the sen-sors and computing power further enrich the experience with these advanced interactions. The user's experience may be enhanced with audio augmenta-tions, creating three-dimensional soundscapes through headsets or external sound systems simulating the auditory qualities of the virtual elements as they might interact with the real environment with the real context. Some forms of MR include haptic augmentations through wearable devices like gloves, vests, jackets, full-body suits, or robotic armatures to provide real-time tactile feedback to the user as if interacting with a real rather than virtual object.

Where Is the Opportunity?

Traditionally, a designer is required to cognitively and haptically transform an inherently three-dimensional idea to a two-dimensional representation (i.e., a drawing). The viewer is then required to interpret that 2D projection and visually and cognitively interpret it as a 3D scene in his or her own mind. On the surface, digital reality can be seen as an expensive evolution to present abstract ideas to designers, stakeholders, and clients. Critically, however, a shared digital reality requires no interpretation, only sensory immersion.

Evolving expectations and market forces have contributed to an increased use of BIM authoring tools, for all types and scales of projects. As a result, there is already a fertile ground for model-based communication throughout the design process and with all the aforementioned stakeholders. Due to the increasing power of these authoring tools and the ubiquity of mobile devices with ever-increasing hardware performance, the effort and steps necessary to publish and share those models via VR/AR/MR environments have dramatically decreased. Every current major BIM authoring tool can now export a model, with literally one click of the mouse, for consumption on a variety of computer

Virtual Reality (VR):
Completely immersive environment with no relation to real environment.

Augmented Reality (AR):
Overlay of digital information within the field of view of real environment. Limited interactivity with digital overlay elements.

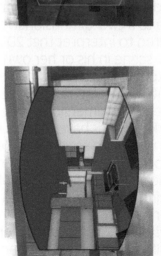

Mixed or Merged Reality (MR):
Overlay and spatial synchronization of digital information within the field of view of the real environment, allowing high-degree of interactivity of digital elements and interplay with real ones.

FIGURE 7.6 Mixed or merged, hybrid, or expanded reality (MR/HR/XR) technology.

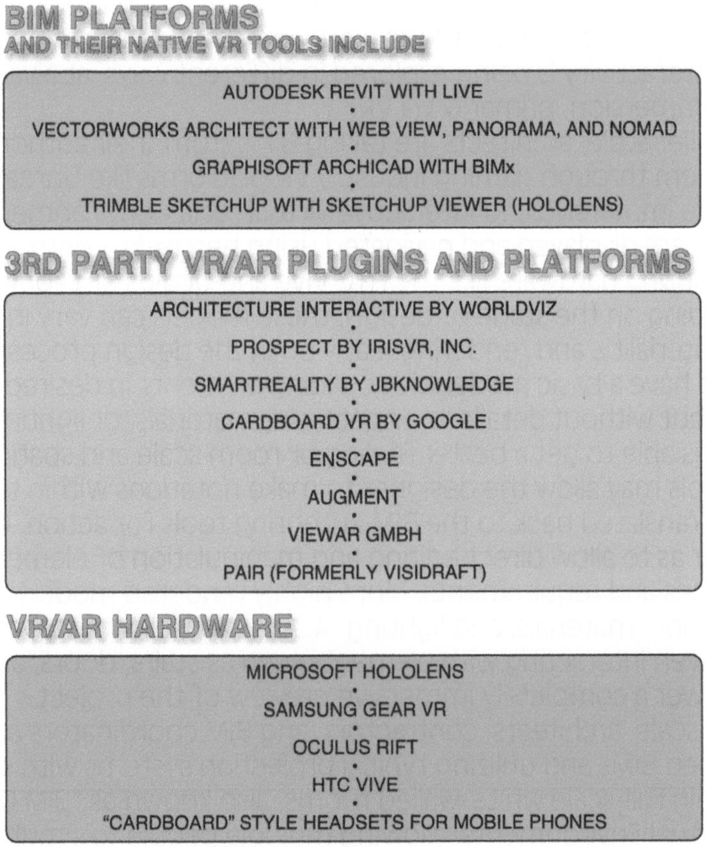

BIM PLATFORMS
AND THEIR NATIVE VR TOOLS INCLUDE

AUTODESK REVIT WITH LIVE
•
VECTORWORKS ARCHITECT WITH WEB VIEW, PANORAMA, AND NOMAD
•
GRAPHISOFT ARCHICAD WITH BIMx
•
TRIMBLE SKETCHUP WITH SKETCHUP VIEWER (HOLOLENS)

3RD PARTY VR/AR PLUGINS AND PLATFORMS

ARCHITECTURE INTERACTIVE BY WORLDVIZ
•
PROSPECT BY IRISVR, INC.
•
SMARTREALITY BY JBKNOWLEDGE
•
CARDBOARD VR BY GOOGLE
•
ENSCAPE
•
AUGMENT
•
VIEWAR GMBH
•
PAIR (FORMERLY VISIDRAFT)

VR/AR HARDWARE

MICROSOFT HOLOLENS
•
SAMSUNG GEAR VR
•
OCULUS RIFT
•
HTC VIVE
•
"CARDBOARD" STYLE HEADSETS FOR MOBILE PHONES

FIGURE 7.7 A summary of current VR/AR/MR options.

platforms and devices (Figure 7.7). There is also a plethora of third-party applications, supplementing the functionality of major modeling platforms and providing VR/AR platforms for creation, transmission, storage, and viewing of models. These solutions may present models with specific software applications and/or hardware, or using general web-based technologies (such as WebVR) and inexpensive stereoscopic headset accessories for mobile devices.

From a design perspective, digital realities are becoming a new instrument of delivery, as well as an integral part of all stages of the design process. In the beginning of the design process, being immersive gives the viewer, whether designer, collaborator, or client, the ability to experience important design aspects—volume, views, circulation, proximity, lighting, color, and materiality. Immersive views can also mitigate regulatory decisions by allowing planning and building officials to see the effects of a design in context. In turn, the viewer can make decisions about the proposed design with an understanding unlike a series of flat, 2D drawings, or even 3D models projected onto a flat monitor. Currently, this type of interactivity is being explored in different ways, at a variety of different levels of immersion, primarily via VR.

At the smaller scale, architects are taking BIMs from their authoring tools and processing them through gaming industry VR platforms like Unreal Engine and Unity to create immersive and interactive virtual reality environments. These environments are displayed and navigated using headsets, controllers, and supporting computing hardware like the HTC Vive and Oculus Rift for individual users. Depending on the stage of design, these models can vary in constructive detail, materiality, and rendering. Early on in the design process, it may be enough to have a basic model with building elements in desired locations and extents, but without detailed connections, materials, or lighting displayed. The designer is able to get a better feeling of room scale and spatial relations. The virtual tools may allow the designer to make notations within the virtual space, to be translated back to the BIM authoring tools for action. Or they may even go so far as to allow direct editing and manipulation of elements to meet desired changes and requirements. More highly rendered models, with accurate construction, materials, and lighting, would allow clients to walk through the project, even interacting with elements such as stairs, doors, and windows, giving the viewer a completely immersive preview of the project.

At a larger scale, architects, contractors, and BIM coordinators are taking the same processed BIMs and utilizing typical projection systems with specialized software within full-scale white-walled rooms, also known as "BIM CAVEs" (Cave Automatic Virtual Environments) allowing multiple people to simultaneously view the model at once, to scale, and coordinate multiple disciplines and their elements prior to construction. These "VR light" environments typical trade off the ability to have a sophisticated immersive and interactive environment benefiting the experience of a single individual with a simpler immersive display for a congregational visual experience.

More and more architects and contractors are experimenting with AR/MR to cross past the boundary of a completely insular virtual environment to leverage the real world in the display of design and construction information. Today, companies like Gilbane Building Company, Mortenson Construction, Martin Bros., and BNBuilders are focused on leveraging AR/MR to augment or even replace the traditional fabrication from 2D drawing process with finished process models projected into the real space alongside the materials/components (Figure 7.8). This enables a laborer to interact, in real scale and space, with no need to interpret abstract 2D drawings and work at matching the real results with the virtual models. This is quite compelling, but what about earlier in the process? How can AR/MR really impact design by architects and engineers?

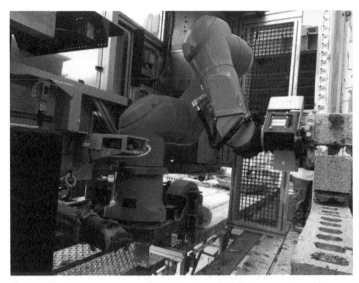

FIGURE 7.8 An example of robotic fabrication/assembly in situ. Workers and machines undertake fabrication directly from digital models rather than interpreting 2D drawings.

Image courtesy of Zak Podkaminer, Construction Robotics.

One could speculate that AR/MR can have meaningful impact in the design process by providing designers with CAD/BIM displays and tools that operate in the existing field of vision of a site or building project. Imagine an architect able to don a DAQURI Smart Helmet, Microsoft HoloLens, or Magic Leap Lightwear, while walking a site or building in which the project is meant to be built, and having all the BIM tools like Revit or Vectorworks available, enabling the construction of virtual models in situ. Ideally, the AR/MR hardware and software would be able to accurately snap or lock the virtual model in the proper scale, space, and perspective, and allow the user to reference existing elements as anchors to virtual elements. The designer could move through real space and the virtual design would be smoothly and consistently translated to maintain a correct relationship to the referenced reality. In addition, real-time AR data feeds could provide contextual graphic overlays of important mapping, building code, demographic, and climate information to utilize during decision-making processes.

Computational Design and Visual Programming Languages

Projects of enormous scale and mind-boggling complexity are nothing new to the world of architecture. After all, buildings and complexes like the Colosseum, the Pantheon, Parthenon, the Great Pyramids, the Forbidden City, and the great cathedrals of Europe have tested the resolve and skills of designers and builders for eons, designed and constructed without the benefits of electricity, sophisticated computational devices, fueled machinery, or in some cases even without basic literacy. Almost all display extensive design repetition and permutations based on numerous aesthetic, mathematic, and physical factors, leveraging small, simple units as the basis for larger, more complex systems. As an example, the Roman Colosseum is a magnificent embodiment of mathematics, proportion, cultural meaning, and harmonic aesthetics wrapping state-of-the-art building technology (for its time), serving a complex program for delivering a wide variety of live entertainment, at an astounding scale and at times extreme brutality, to large crowds of spectators, year-round. To deliver the project, designers had to deduce and employ logic, or rules, across the spectrum of physical systems to generate coherent, cohesive, and functional results. Rules of proportion for elements like columns and arches were founded on the physical capacity, or limitations, of historic concrete and masonry materials and structural systems, while also influenced by culturally significant styles (Doric, Ionic, Corinthian orders). Intricate geometric and mathematical studies helped fit the proportional, multistory façade system to an ovoid plan, while providing adequate circulation and seating for the human spectators, and keeping them separate from the behind-the-scenes entertainment (Figure 7.9).

FIGURE 7.9 A CADD illustration and BIM model of the Colosseum. Algorithms of proportion and structural logic are encoded in this Roman architectural monument.

Surveying such sophisticated design and construction methodologies, a modern designer can recognize algorithmic-based processes that are common to similarly scaled prominent projects of our era. Today's analogous projects are no less daunting, complex, or sophisticated for today's architect, who may face significant pressures and limitations of resources, time, and economics. In such an atmosphere, getting to the best possible design solution, typically through the study of multiple iterations, requires speed as much as competence. Computers, paired with the right software tools, are an opportunity to harness such volumes of complexity at great speeds, but also require considerable skill to wield in order to get the best results.

Computational Design

Computational design leverages computing technology in the application of algorithms (sets of rules governing calculations or logical operations) to manipulate simple elements or components to create larger, more complex digital forms per user-specified variables, or parameters. As a simple example, computational design can be used to automatically create a complex pattern of randomly sized openings in a façade, given user-defined parameters:

▫ The extents of the façade

▫ Upper and lower limits of opening size

▫ Preferred geometry of the dimensional modules

At a far more complex level, computational design can be used to harmonize and optimize the structural and cladding systems of an asymmetrical layout for a sports stadium in an arid climate, with tools to determine least number of panel variations, most optimal structural element orientations, and most efficient layout of connections between the two systems to accommodate structural integrity and thermal expansion. With enough computational power, such design methodologies can even be applied on an urban planning scale, redesigning entire sections of a city with optimal mixes of use, open space, building heights, and densities with factors including socioeconomic demographics, population growth, traffic patterns, and environmental influences. Computational design offers architects the ability to create and analyze multiple iterations with great speed, letting the designer focus on making value judgments on the results and narrowing down preferred options. However, it is also necessary for the designer to design the algorithms themselves—determining appropriate inputs (parameters), configuring formulas and/or processes to use the inputs, and selecting means of displaying the results—requiring computational knowledge, the ability to write these logics in computer code.

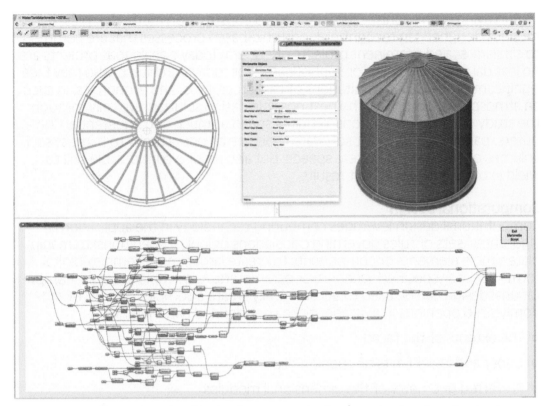

FIGURE 7.10 An illustration of a VPL (visual programming language) network and output.
Image courtesy of Vectorworks, Inc.

The threshold for computational design has been lowered significantly in recent years with the creation of new computing languages (such as Python, Ruby, and Swift) and the use of graphic elements connected to scripting or programming elements (Figure 7.10), also known as visual programming languages (VPLs), enabling an explosion of formal exploration by designers who are more attuned to visual development than text-based coding.

Visual Programming Languages

Many of the major CAD platforms used over the past 30 years had a means for end users to automate functionality without the need to know development code like C++, Visual Basic, or .NET. With more natural language scripting languages, users have been able to write simple routines automating tedious, repetitive tasks, or dive into manipulating shapes and forms based on user-defined rules or formulas. But many of these scripting languages (like AutoLISP, GDL, and MiniPascal) still required an advanced level of understanding in order to make advanced computational designs work.

Software companies have since provided end users with another means of manipulating their functionality to get dynamic results. These visual programming languages (VPLs), also known as graphical scripting, enable users who "think visually" to actively engage the creation of complex algorithms to automate processes for an application. Such graphical scripting has even become accessible to children, such as MIT's Scratch programming environment and robotic construction toys, notably LEGO® Mindstorms® (Figure 7.11).

The visual elements of a VPL are typically based on diagrammatic notations, where functions are displayed as 2D graphic "nodes," like a rectangle, and linked together in a particular sequence with "wires" that connect specific inputs and outputs from each of the nodes. A collection of nodes and wires creates

MODERN CAD/BIM
VISUAL PROGRAMMING LANGUAGES

GENERATIVE COMPONENTS FOR MICROSTATION BY BENTLEY SYSTEMS
·
GRASSHOPPER 3D FOR RHINOCEROS 3D BY ROBERT McNEEL & ASSOCIATES
·
DYNAMO FOR REVIT AND MAYA BY AUTODESK, INC.
·
MARIONETTE FOR VECTORWORKS BY VECTORWORKS, INC.

OTHER VISUAL PROGRAMMING LANGUAGES

SCRATCH BY MIT
·
CAMELEON BY OLIVIER CUGNON DE SÉVRICOURT AND VINCENT TARIEL
·
REAKTOR BY NATIVE INSTRUMENTS
·
NXT-G BY THE LEGO GROUP

ACADEMIC PROGRAMS
FOR COMPUTATIONAL DESIGN AS APPLIED TO ARCHITECTURE

MSC AND PhD OF COMPUTATIONAL DESIGN AT CARNEGIE MELLON
UNIVERSITY
·
THE DESIGN AND COMPUTATION GROUP AT MIT SCHOOL OF
ARCHITECTURE + PLANNING
·
COMPUTATIONAL DESIGN STUDIO, M. ARCH. AT CORNELL UNIVERSITY
COLLEGE OF ARCHITECTURE, ART AND PLANNING (AAP)
·
MSC ARCHITECTURAL COMPUTATION AT THE UNIVERSITY COLLEGE
LONDON BARTLETT SCHOOL OF ARCHITECTURE
·
DIGITAL BUILDING LAB AT THE GEORGIA TECH SCHOOL OF
ARCHITECTURE
·
INSTITUTE OF COMPUTATIONAL DESIGN AT THE UNIVERSITY OF
STUTTGART
·
ACADIA

FIGURE 7.11 A list of common VPL applications and academic teaching programs.

a "network," providing a graphical representation of multiline ASCII code typically used by computer programmers. In most cases, the VPLs provide nodes that represent interactive inputs, or parameters, for the network creator or another end user, to manipulate the results based on end user-defined values. These values may include parameters like height, width, or number of divisions, or more complex inputs like maximum angle of incidence, user-selected base geometries, or even links to other objects like a digital image in the form of a JPEG or PNG.

Where Is the Opportunity?

As a result of VPLs, designers have experimented with more complex design strategies to create highly variegated forms that respond to multiple inputs and constraints (Figure 7.12). The automation allows the designer to quickly test and evaluate multiple variables and outcomes before deciding on a final design. In addition to built projects, these tools become important pedagogical resources,

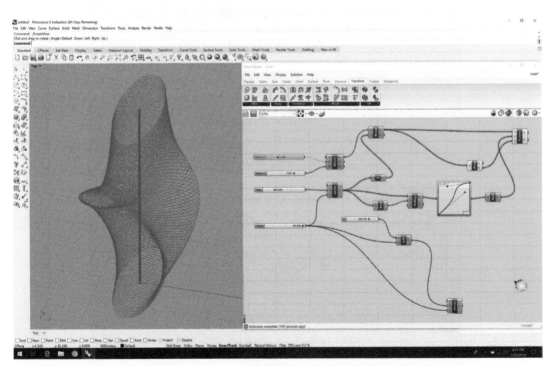

FIGURE 7.12 This is an example of a simple Grasshopper script in Rhino3D v6 that takes an arbitrary oval, copies vertically by a user-input multiple, then twists the entire stack by a user-defined variable.

Image by Jeffrey W. Ouellette.

platforms for learning about the development of design processes and how these technologies can capture inputs from any number and type of sources and affect outcomes, whether realistic or purely theoretical. Architects and designers such as Peter Eisenman, Adrian Smith, Greg Lynn, and Nathan Miller, as well as firms such as Zaha Hadid, NBBJ, HOK, and SOM, have been designing and building many high-profile projects that were based on computational design methodologies and VPLs for a variety of tools, to dramatic effect. The VPLs and the tools connected to them also open up the design process to more dynamic exploration of various simulation and analysis regimes, whether related to environmental factors like lighting, wind speed, solar gain, and other climatic conditions, or physical conditions of strength, geometric optimization, and fabrication constraints (Figure 7.13).

Nathan Miller, founder and managing director of Proving Ground, reflects on how mature the idea of using this method of programming has become,

FIGURE 7.13 The Miller Hull Partnership employed visual programming to optimize the photovoltaic solar array, a significant design element, for their Bullitt Center project in Seattle, Washington.

Image courtesy of the Miller Hull Partnership.

especially as an aid in democratizing tool making to address increasingly complex design parameters. VPLs allow the end users of technology to customize current software to address particular design workflows, as well as add functionality that might be entirely missing from an out-of-the-box solution. This investment gives the technology end user more ownership in the tools themselves, as well as the results. Examples of this may range from simple scripting of a repetitive task—e.g., creating a location map for a project by taking a snapshot of the site in a Google Maps view and pasting it directly on a cover sheet—to more complex and intricate sets and combinations of scripts—such as developing the optimal shape and extents of shading devices on a midrise building responding to physical parameters and solar orientation/shadow casting over a period of time. The new tools give the designer increasing prowess in developing design solutions that are optimized for aesthetic, economic, operational, and environmental factors.

Miller also notes that to an increasing degree, the ability to master VPLs and apply them to different modes of computational design has become its own recognized discipline and professional specialization in the design world. The skills of an adept computational designer, like Miller and his colleagues, are now highly sought after to address the complexity of projects with large scales, scopes, and number of important design parameters to be collated, rationalized, harmonized, and thoughtfully applied. This is not a mere specialization of applied computer science, but a savvy synthesis of technological innovation with exceptional design skills and intuition. Students in many schools of architecture are now frequently exposed to these tools, ideally learning to harness such technology while concurrently learning about design thinking and processes. Advanced degree programs further explore the intersection of architecture, computer science, and computer engineering as a means to apply algorithm and programming concepts to further the design of the built environment.

However, as Miller observes, the relatively rapid emergence and maturation of computational design has also created cultural friction, challenging the traditionally recognized status quo of design—the mind and genius of the architect as artist and author. It has prompted some backlash due to the implications of significant cultural changes when technology and the ability to collect, analyze, and manipulate large troves of data become so important to the design process. As aesthetically revolutionary some view the history of architecture, others view the datacentric and digitally augmented methodology as a cold attack on a revered culture and institution centered on human inspiration. This issue of culture is significant, particularly as the perception of the architect's intelligence is further challenged by the use of machine learning and artificial intelligence augmented by computational design and VPLs. For the skeptics, these new modes are best suited to optimize tedious processes like tiling, panelization, semirandom pattern creation, structural/architectural system optimization, or even dynamic lighting display controls, to name a few. This can relegate those proficient few into a limited "trade role" where their skills are focused on a subset of the larger process and problem of design. Nevertheless, a new generation of designers, architectural associates, and architects are more open to new software and methods, embracing the possibilities of utilizing different tools, processes, and aesthetics for the entire scope of design and even construction, with potentially richer and more diverse design outcomes.

Finally, Miller sees an important, if not subversive, impact on the relationship between vendors, their technology, and end users. Open source tools and algorithms that can be connected or embedded in proprietary platforms via VPLs help end users force new modes of creation and interoperability between tools. In some cases, it is possible to work around the traditional API (application programming interface) or SDK (software development kit) schemas that require a higher knowledge of low-level programming and integration with platforms. End users can focus more on what they want to accomplish without the possible technical restrictions of a single product or vendor, right out of the box.

As complex, perhaps even cold, as it may seem to some, computational design and visual programming languages are tools that will play an ever-increasing part in the design and BIM process. This is only natural as the profession becomes more digital and data-centric. As always, cultural attitudes within the profession will be further influenced and mitigated by the larger cultural and technological influences outside the profession. There will be ample opportunities for those who see a positive future, rather than a bleak one, in the implementation of techniques and strategies that harness computing rather than fight against it, or wearily march on in spite of it.

LiDAR, Photogrammetry, and Point Clouds

Also known as 3D or laser scanning, **LiDAR** (LIght Detection And Ranging) is a package of instrumentation where a laser is shone on a surface and the distance and color of a specific point is then returned to the instrument's sensors, repeated millions of times, every x/y/z coordinate and color value stored, with user-controlled scanning density (Figures 7.14 and 7.15). The technology was originally developed in the 1960s, combining new lasers with radar systems, and applied to meteorological research. Since then, the parallel evolution of laser, optic, GPS, and computing technologies have dramatically reduced the complexity, size, and cost of systems to the point where entry level systems—including scanning hardware, accessories, processing software and manufacturer maintenance contracts—can be purchased for about US$50,000; more substantial systems cost about US$100,000. For those not willing to purchase

L.I.D.A.R. SYSTEMS
FOR BUILDING INDUSTRY

FARO TECHNOLOGIES, INC.
·
TOPCON POSITIONING SYSTEMS, INC.
·
LEICA GEOSYSTEMS
·
PHOENIX LIDAR SYSTEMS
·
PARACOSM, INC.

PHOTOGRAMMETRY SYSTEMS

RECAP BY AUTODESK, INC.
·
ACUTE3D BY BENTLEY SYSTEMS, INC.
·
PIX4DMAPPER PRO, PIX4DBIM AND PIX4DMODEL BY PIX4D SA

APS AND TERRAIN TOOLS BY MENCI SOFTWARE
·
PHOTO TO 3D MODEL BY VECTORWORKS, IINC.

FIGURE 7.14 Table of LiDAR and photogrammetry hardware and software options.

FIGURE 7.15 Point cloud, LiDAR-generated scan model of heritage tree directly integrated in BIM authoring file.

Scan courtesy of True World Services, Austin, Texas.

and maintain their own equipment, services to scan existing buildings and landscapes can be acquired for as little as US$1,500 per day for simple setups to as much as US$2,500 per day for complex contexts requiring numerous scans from multiple stations and setups.

Photogrammetry is as old as the technology of photography itself; the dimensions of objects and their locations in space can be determined through analyzing distances in relation to perspective projections of a still image and a few known base points and measurements located within the image's field of view. Digital imaging and computerized image analysis has automated this methodology, making it faster and more accurate for many different scales and complexities of geometry. Images can be obtained using digital cameras that are handheld, attached to tripods, cars, or, the most popular current device, unmanned aerial vehicles (UAVs, or drones). The resulting 2D images are then "stitched" together in a 3D space to form a model based on the analysis.

Whether using LiDAR or photogrammetry, the resulting data is processed into point clouds, millions of colored pixels properly arranged in three dimensions to infer surfaces and volumes. These point clouds are then used by modeling software as references or backgrounds, and can be superimposed with intelligent BIM objects or simple 3D planar or solid geometry. The evolution of computing power and simultaneous development of open source software for processing and importing point cloud data into modeling software has sparked a very recent explosion of support for point clouds in all the major BIM authoring tools.

Where Is the Opportunity?

Due to the lowering of costs, it is now easier than ever to collect data representing "as-built" conditions of a building or site before starting the design of a project. This data can be highly accurate and made immediately available in a meaningful way to an architect's preferred platform without a great deal of labor in manual measurement, interpretation, and input.

The two different data collection technologies are not so much competing as finding a complementary balance based on respective capabilities. LiDAR technology is generally very accurate and comprehensive due to the laser methodology, but because of the size of the instrumentation and reliance on stability of the sensors, it is a better fit for stationary applications. For exterior building and site surveys, it may prove difficult to get comprehensive coverage on tall structures or large sites without access to vantage points or stations above the ground. In such cases, the mobility of UAVs, or drones, with high-fidelity cameras mounted on them can be advantageous. Interiors of buildings present the reverse scenario where the effectiveness of drones is limited by close confines, but LiDAR units can be repositioned in a matter of minutes and resulting scans accurately aligned and registered to each other.

While LiDAR may seem exotic or limited to large-scale surveys of public or commercial projects, it is beginning to be within reach even of small or residential projects where warranted. And the technology is not limited to built applications. Lévy Kohlhaas Architects engaged True World Services to laser scan a large heritage tree whose canopy was a design consideration; architect and owner were concerned that the early design iterations of a single-family home might conflict with some of the adjacent tree's branches. Moreover, Austin, Texas, has a heritage tree ordinance that would prohibit significant damage to the 36" (0.91 m) trunk diameter ash tree's canopy. The laser scan was completed in an hour or two with point cloud postprocessed and delivered online the same day, and was far faster and more accurate than an earlier attempt to conventionally measure and model the tree's structure. As a result, architect and client could make an informed design decision, far preferable to simply building the house and hoping for the best, or compromising the design unnecessarily for a false positive.

At Pix4D SA, Julian Norton, business development, sees the use of photogrammetry and image analysis as having greater future potential than LiDAR systems because of its flexibility and the continued advances in self-navigation technologies for UAVs, especially for interior conditions. He also sees the advancement of optics and digital imagery, including 360-degree image capture devices and hybrid LiDAR/imaging systems as increasing the value for photogrammetry, image analysis, and processing. Add to this cloud-based processing and storage of immense amounts of data with crowdsourcing of 3D data collection and the potential of accurately modeling a virtual copy of the real world is almost at arm's reach. At that point, context data for urban or building design from the right government agency or service provider may only be a click away.

Artificial Intelligence (AI)

A common trope of the "golden age" of science fiction is that of a new sentient intelligence emerging not from other biological species, but from the increasingly advanced technology humanity has created. Typically, these speculations involve the struggle to reconcile the autonomous will of such new beings, such as Isaac Asimov's *I, Robot*, Philip K. Dick's *Do Androids Dream of Electric Sheep?*, or Arthur C. Clarke's *2001: A Space Odyssey*, and the interests of their creators. It was taken as a given that these new artificial intelligences were the logical and inevitable consequences of humans' technological development to harness science and improve life by easing the burden of work, repetitive and menial tasks, or enhance our own evolution by dramatically increasing our knowledge capacity and decision-making capabilities.

In the service of this sentiment, an accelerating body of work has been done in the past 20 years in the development and application of general artificial intelligence (AI). In the last few years, many research institutions, as well as private companies like Google, Microsoft, and IBM, have invested a great deal of time, money, and human ingenuity into leveraging advances in computation to take on numerous tasks of receiving, processing, analyzing, and acting on copious amounts of data for any number of disciplines, including but not limited to astronomy, biology, climatology, medicine, logistics, media, and statistics (Figure 7.16). Usually, the intent is to automate and accelerate the processing of information in a fraction of the time that it would normally take a human. This allows speedier production and analysis of results to create permutations to solutions that can be more readily judged appropriate or correct.

Architecture, the design and construction of buildings, is fraught with data and decision-making challenges. Even beyond the subjective factors of aesthetics, there are often large amounts of information—building codes, geotechnical conditions, climate, demographics, economics, building tech-nology, schedule, materials, and so on—that must be considered and processed to achieve what the designer and client believe is the best possible solution. Even the determination of what is "best" can be quite subjective, weighed by aesthetics against all the other information to find an acceptable, though maybe not always optimal, resolution. Throughout its history, architecture has seen innovations in developing tools to help this process, including perspec-tive drawing, scale models, heliodons, climate data, product testing, and now CAD and BIM.

Beyond the relatively simple computational design discussed earlier, the recent trends are harnessing even greater computing power to approach design in a data-centric, problem-solving manner that reflects the "big data" or "data mining" inno-vations being used in other industries. While the use of AI in architectural design may conjure pejorative notions of computers quickly and automatically designing Frank Lloyd Wright-style shopping malls or Neo-Roman palaces for totalitarian nationalists, the actual goals are less subjective and aesthetic, and based more on assistance in decision making for more pragmatic and routine concerns.

COMMERCIAL ARTIFICIAL INTELLIGENCE/ MACHINE LEARNING PLATFORMS

WATSON BY IBM
·
SAFFRON BY INTEL CORP. & SAFFRON TECHNOLOGY, INC.
·
TENSORFLOW AND CLOUD MACHINE LEARNING BY GOOGLE, INC.
·
AMAZON AI BY AMAZON WEB SERVICES, INC.

FIGURE 7.16 Common AI/ML (artificial intelligence/machine learning) commercial platforms.

The general concept of artificial intelligence (AI) is actually very broad, encompassing a number of important subtopics and specific areas of complex computational research and development, including neural networks, human speech recognition, gaming theory, natural language processing, and others.

Where Is the Opportunity?

By utilizing the principles of machine learning, where a computing platform can learn how to independently make valid decisions through analysis of previous situations and results (Figure 7.17), can architects further automate mundane or complex processes with an infallible, or at least less error prone, autonomous intelligence, removing the requirement of human interaction and decision making at every step and iteration?

In the above-noted discussion with Proving Grounds' Nathan Miller, the application of artificial intelligence and machine learning is further enhanced with computational design and visual programming languages. More tools are being developed to help those without the deep computer science knowledge or computer engineering skills to leverage AI and ML systems through simplified user interfaces.

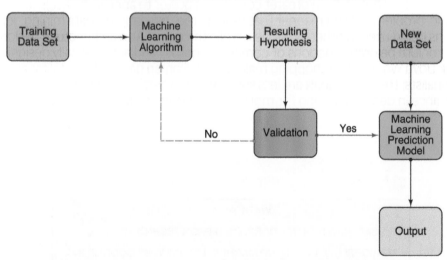

FIGURE 7.17 A flow chart diagram of the artificial intelligence/machine learning (AI/ML) process, whereby training and then later data sets are algorithmically tested to produce a refined computational output.

Future potential. Emerging applications of machine learning are beginning to have an impact on everyday life; opening up an opportunity to leverage ML for design analysis and simulation. One can speculate that capabilities like Amazon's, directed at predicting choices and decisions, could be applied to occupant behavior in buildings such that designers could better anticipate and plan for the interaction between complex mechanical and electrical systems and the people who use them, thereby improving building energy efficiency and performance.

On a practice-wide level, lessons from past projects could be distilled and applied to future projects. Teamwork between design professionals could be improved through improved and anticipatory knowledge gathering and management, for better communication and transparency. Consistent data and vetted analysis of past projects would be needed to "feed the machine" and render good results. This could in turn free designers to focus more on those subjective design decisions that artificial intelligence and machine learning are—for the moment—ill equipped to make.

Some less creative tasks that could be shouldered by AI/ML might include clash detection, narrowing options for product selection for planned spaces, and coordinating project specifications, and models could be improved whereby software applications "knew" where an object is placed, automatically coordinating all subsequent data and operations.

In pursuing her PhD in construction engineering and project management at the University of Texas at Austin, Li Wang, VDC coordinator at Austin Commercial, a Texas-based general contractor, investigated the use of machine learning and data mining techniques to support the process of design coordination between building systems. Her thesis proposed leveraging previous BIM-based designs, the inevitable conflicts between domain models, and the resulting resolutions, from a number of past projects (Figure 7.18). Dr. Wang proposed a system that could automatically examine similar new circumstances, sort through predefined and learned rules and constraints, and determine a small number of possible solutions for the architect and other design collaborators to choose from. This could significantly reduce the amount of time and resources spent on clash detection between systems and determining viable solutions. It would also have the added benefit of leveraging the knowledge of a few more experienced personnel and capturing it in a system that could be more widely used by a larger number of novices during training and early project experiences.

But for such a system to work, three primary factors must exist:

1. A large number of previous instances.

2. Consistent documentation of instances and resolutions.

3. A formal and consistent ontology used to describe and categorize the many different types of coordination issues and their resolutions.

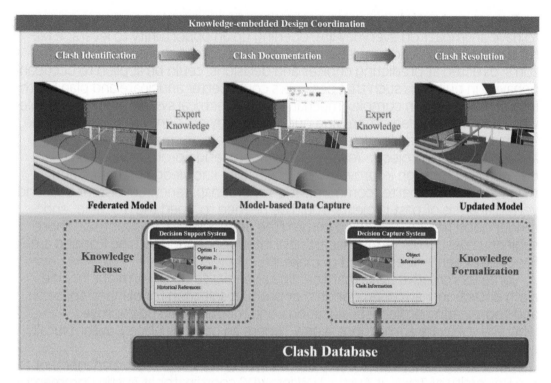

FIGURE 7.18 Dr. Li Wang's research work is focused on the use of machine learning and data mining techniques to support the process of design coordination between building systems. *Image courtesy of Li Wang.*

AI systems depend on the consistent quality of large amounts of data to develop learning skills and the means of writing their own rules in decision making based on patterns that emerge from a data set. While able to create a proof-of-concept for her thesis, Dr. Wang also revealed the important challenges for providing practical commercial AI solutions. These challenges included:

▫ A resistance to collecting data in the midst of the project delivery process. People were more often focused on identifying a problem, solving it, and moving on as quickly as possible than to consciously collect and curate the results of the process for future research.

▫ The larger cultural, financial, and litigious resistance to share such data and leverage it beyond a particular project. Industry stakeholders may think that sharing may expose unique secrets to success or weaknesses that competitors might exploit to their advantage. There is also a concern that sharing further exposes a person or firm to liability and risk of fault, where data is seen as ammunition or proof of incompetency.

❏ The lack of data ontology and collection standards. The US building industry is notorious for the lack of implementing nonmandated standards of any kind, whether a small practice or a national or international organization. Dr. Wang's ideas require a codified common language, nomenclature, and method for identifying, collecting, and the curation of data.

Unlike financial transactions like stock trading or record keeping for service delivery like health care, the building industry currently lacks consistent data at a scale for AI systems to be effective. Recognizing these shortcomings, however, can be a first step in rectifying that deficiency. It may also provide opportunities for private business, regulatory bodies, and industry stakeholders to innovate as well as take on the cultural challenges of overcoming such hurdles, leading to solutions that add productivity, reduce costs and liability, and improve the overall value of the resulting product.

Conclusion

The current trends of advanced technology being applied to BIM and design processes are really the adoption of previous technologies that have finally reached maturation, such that ease of use and accessible costs are making it easier to implement them. That doesn't make the technology any less exciting or useful to current practitioners. Rather, accessible technology encourages greater adoption as risks are lowered, processes are refined, and use becomes less esoteric. Consider where CAD systems were 30 years ago (large, expensive, dedicated, single-use terminals) and how pervasive they are today.

This begs the question, "What's next?" What are forthcoming technological innovations that might be applied to the design process? What about the Internet of Things (IoT) with full-time, real-time connectivity to sensors of various kinds? One might imagine such sensor arrays providing architects with meaningful data for responsive, context-specific designs. There are now numerous nascent developments regarding use of product manufacturing methodologies, known as design for manufacture and assembly (DfMA). Imagine buildings put together like automobiles by robots, or assembled with larger premanufactured components and assemblies that "snap together" on-site, rather than the traditional "stick-built" construction techniques. Then there is 3D printing and computer controlled (CNC) multiaxis milling to fabricate complex parts directly from digital design models, using virtually any material. Subsurface imaging, including X-ray, MRI, sonar, and ground-penetrating radar, provides more extensive and accurate surveys of existing underground conditions to better inform designers, engineers, and builders and reduce the risk of finding the unexpected at an inopportune moment.

Ultimately, we must recognize that the profession and the design process will continue to evolve as technological innovations meaningfully applied become valuable. We must not hesitate to explore, experiment, fail—and try again. Architects can avoid the romantic nostalgia trap that technology is antithetical to architectural artistry. Being thoughtful, intelligent, and educated consumers of technology will serve architects, and therefore their clients and society at large.

Writing is a learning experience, and a test. Like design, it's more a matter of discovering one among many possible truths, rather than merely committing to paper what is already known. In writing, as in design, one sets about to solve a problem whose boundaries are not fully known—here I mean boundaries like the metes and bounds of a site, or the boundary conditions of an engineering problem. In other words, not boundaries like a limit that the laws of nature have demanded, but a thoughtful yet arbitrary circumference set by agreement in order to make a problem more tractable. And as with design, the boundaries of a "writing problem" are called into question by the act of writing. *Have I strayed too far from the topic, or should the topic be shifted, broadened or narrowed, or deformed into another shape altogether?*

When at the onset I designed the boundaries of this book, I already knew a lot about the topic, but clearly not everything that wound up on the page. In writing as in design, there's obviously some measure of expressing existing knowledge, but that is just the starting point. The first steps given by what's already known might provide insights into the general direction of the work, but that preliminary knowledge and the boundaries it suggests are by no means definitive. Perhaps a better way to think about *a priori* knowledge in the context of a design problem—or a written work—is that it helps provisionally frame the questions. It doesn't give the answers. Or as Jeffrey Siegel, an engineering professor of mine once put it, engineering school doesn't teach you to be an engineer; it just teaches you what you will need to learn in order to become one. So it is with design, or writing. The knowledge we start with merely gets us started.

Writing—and design—is also a test. Of endurance, surely, but that's not what I'm pointing to. If approached with intellectual honesty and a small measure of courage, both are a trial of assumptions and prejudices, little crucibles where ideas can be forged and put to the fire. Some ideas recoil from this *auto-da-fé*, others succumb to the heat, and a few are alloyed into something stronger.

For most of my professional career it so happened that I have come to test *how* to design, and BIM has been a foundational factor in that process. To be clear,

I didn't set out to discover a new design manifesto, nor do I particularly think that this book is one. It stumbled upon me. I came to life early and to architecture late; when I started out in the profession I had a concern for finding a voice. At the time, I thought that voice would *look like something*, have a distinct outward appearance, a recognizable (and therefore necessarily repetitive) form. Indeed, I imagined it to be a formal vocabulary—an architectural shtick, if you will. It turns out that like most designers I have certain shapes or forms or figured ground diagrams that for unqualified reasons hold a visual appeal for me. So what? The idiosyncratic, sculptural part of architecture—what confuses most laymen and has them lump us in with artists—is perhaps initially the most charming or attractive part of architecture, and in the end perhaps the least important. In my view, it's the icing on the cake. So is a particular kind of intellectual rigor, like those early twentieth-century "rules" for architecture, be they Bauhaus or that Swiss fellow. That is to the mind what eye candy is to the visual sense. Stimulating, maybe even titillating, but all about outcome. The problem with having a particular visual or intellectual vocabulary is that of *sameness*. Whether formal or theoretical, that kind of design voice is concerned with outcomes, or appearances. And why not? After all, aren't outcomes and appearances why we're hired?

And yet, listen to Antoine de Saint-Exupéry: *L'essentiel est invisible pour les yeux* ("What is essential is invisible to the eyes"). In architecture as in poetry, what is truly essential is the process; a powerful process will have you create something worthy of your humanity. The critic Konrad Fielder understood art as an alternative cognitive process, another way of thinking. While he acknowledged the societal value of art objects, the artistic byproduct was far less important to him than the process from which it emerged. For Fiedler an art object was only artistically interesting insofar as it was revelatory of the process of its creation; art for him was not an intellectual process but a participatory one. In a similar vein, insofar as architects are like artists, it's not because we make forms—that's just a superficial resemblance. It's because like artists we have a process, and the value of the work is in exercising that process. The rest, that's just product.

Organisms on earth developed in specific environments and have evolved specific responses accordingly. For example, why do we only see in the visible spectrum (from 0.3 and 0.7 micrometers), a tiny fraction of the entire electromagnetic spectrum? It turns out that our atmosphere is opaque to large parts of the solar radiation spectrum except for a few frequencies, occurring at atmospheric windows: optical light, infrared radiation, and to a certain degree micro- and short radio waves. Of that, fully half of the sun's energy that reaches the earth's surface is in the visible spectrum. If you were going to evolve eyes that used the sun's radiation to illuminate your environment, they would naturally capitalize on the most abundant available energy source, which due to a fluke of our atmospheric composition happens to be what we call

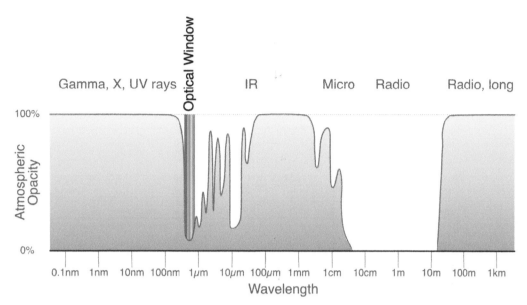

FIGURE A.1 The atmosphere's opacity to the electromagnetic spectrum varies with the wavelength of the radiation. Human eyes, like many animals', are responsive to the optical window that we see as "visible light." Based on a lecture illustration by Professor Kevin Luhman, Penn State Department of Astronomy & Astrophysics.

visible light. And while I hardly subscribe to "intelligent design," evolution offers a biological analogy to design: forms and systems exist entirely in response to outside inputs.

And thus the crux of this book: design is richer and likelier to be successful when it is responsive to its environment—be it site, budget, climate, constructability, or gravity regime. BIM offers designers an opportunity to gather information embedded in the architectural model and make use of it through all phases of design. To use BIM merely as an expedited production platform misses an important opportunity to bring new depth to design processes.

François Lévy
Austin, Texas

FIGURE A.1 The atmosphere is opaque to the electromagnetic spectrum, with the exception of the "windows." Human eyes, like many animals', are responsive to the optical window that we see as "visible light." Based on a lecture illustration by Professor Edward Robson, Penn State Department of Astronomy & Astrophysics.

visible light. And while I hardly subscribe to "intelligent design," evolution offers a biological analogy to design, forms, and systems that entail impressive results.

And thus the crux of this book: design is better and likelier to be successful when it is responsive to its environment—be it site, budget, climate, construction, political, or gravity regime. BIM offers designers an opportunity to gather information embedded in the architectural model and make use of it through all phases of design, to reuse and reuse—as an expedited production platform and as an impressive opportunity to bring new data to design processes.

François Lévy
Austin, Texas